GRIMSBY
STREETS

GRIMSBY STREETS

Emma Lingard

PEN & SWORD
HISTORY

First published in Great Britain in 2017
and reprinted in 2018 by
Pen & Sword HISTORY
An imprint of Pen & Sword Books Ltd
Yorkshire – Philadelphia

Copyright © Emma Lingard, 2017, 2018
ISBN: 978 1 47387 601 9

Printed and bound in the UK by CPI Group (UK) Ltd, Croydon, CR0 4YY

Pen & Sword Books Limited incorporates the imprints of Atlas, Archaeology, Aviation, Discovery, Family History, Fiction, History, Maritime, Military, Military Classics, Politics, Select, Transport, True Crime, Air World, Frontline Publishing, Leo Cooper, Remember When, Seaforth Publishing, The Praetorian Press, Wharncliffe Local History, Wharncliffe Transport, Wharncliffe True Crime and White Owl.

For a complete list of Pen & Sword titles please contact
PEN & SWORD BOOKS LIMITED
47 Church Street, Barnsley, South Yorkshire, S70 2AS, England
E-mail: enquiries@pen-and-sword.co.uk • Website: www.pen-and-sword.co.uk
Or
PEN AND SWORD BOOKS
1950 Lawrence Rd, Havertown, PA 19083, USA
E-mail: Uspen-and-sword@casematepublishers.com
Website: www.penandswordbooks.com

Contents

Dedication

Dedicated with love to my parents Dennis and Carol, whose passion for history ignited my own, my sister Hannah and most of all, my son Tom.

Foreword

Listed are streets within Grimsby. It does include some streets from Scartho, which is now no longer viewed as a village, but as a suburb of the town. However, my reasons for including it are selfish, as it is where I grew up and was where I first began thinking about whom the streets were named after.

The book does include some streets that are no longer in existence, but I felt it was important to include them to prevent them from being lost all together. A majority of the streets were named after prominent people in the town – landowners and politicians, people connected with the growth and development of the port – whose work was enough to warrant them having a highway named after them.

It is the intention of this book to inform the reader of whom those people were and why they were significant to the development of the Victorian town.

Introduction

The Early History of Grimsby

Grimsby, on the east coast of England, has its roots in Scandinavian mythology. Ask any Grimbarian, and they can recall the tale of the Danish fisherman Grim, who rescued Prince Havelok from the stormy sea, and brought him to England, whereon the Prince fell in love and married Goldborough, while Grim founded a town, and lived in an upturned boat.

Whether the tale is fact or fiction, the town seems to have its roots in the Viking ages. The fisherman's name, Grim, linked with the Scandinavian suffix -by, literally means the village or farmstead of Grim. The fact that Grim, or Grimr, is seen as the founder of the town can be seen on the borough seal and in these lines from *The Lay of Havelok the Dane* (lines 743-48):

> And for þat Grim þat place aute
> Þe stede of Grim þe name laute,
> So þat Grimesbi it calle
> Þat þer-offe speken alle;
> Bituene þis and Domesday.

It was also mentioned in *Estoire des Engleis*, written in the twelfth century by Gaimar. He mentions that 20,000 Danes passed by the town on their way to attack York – this was in 866. But in the Icelandic saga, *The Heimskringla*, written circa 1230, no mention is made of the town when discussing the same invasion.

Gillett (1970) refers to a Snorri Stuluson who placed Grimsby within the county of Northumbria and, referring to the 866 raid, says that many place-names within that county were Norwegian. In fact, researching the name Grim finds it is a common Norwegian name, and as we look into the history of the town it has always had strong connections with this country.

To reinforce the Norwegian connection, Gillett references the *Orkneyingers Saga*, which sees a bunch of merchants arrive in Grimsby from Bergen.

Weeks of grimmest walking five
Have we waded through the mud;
In mid-Grimsby where we were
Was no want of mud and mire.

1. Haven Mill, Riverhead.

The lines depict the Haven, and their boats lying in the mud. In fact, the Haven is the reason why settlers came. A tidal creek fed by fresh water springs, it originally stretched as far as where modern day Ainslie Street is, and branched out towards the present day Welholme Avenue.

As we start to delve into the history behind the names of the town's streets, one will also see its ancient roots in the endings of the main town highways. That word is the English suffix -gate, but comes from the Scandinavian word *gata*, meaning street. This suggests the streets named Bargate, Brighowgate, Cartergate, Deansgate, and Wellowgate are borne out of Danish/Norwegian origins, and are therefore ancient highways of the town.

If we go back before the invasion of the Vikings, archaeological evidence according to Bates (18930) shows Romans were here because coins and a boat with a Roman Eagle were found in the vicinity of the current Wheatsheaf pub.

There has been dispute among some over the name Grim, whether it was the name of the Viking founder, and was he Danish or Norwegian, or simply adapted by one or other of the incoming invaders as they sought pastures new. In Celtic times, the area would have come under the Corieltauvi tribe (sometimes referred to as Coritani) and it was Reverend Oliver (1825) who believed that Grim was a Celtic word meaning the residence of a valiant and powerful people.

He also suggests that the town was connected with druid practices, and that there was a stone circle here. No evidence has ever been found, and this may be elaboration on the part of the author.

When the Normans arrived, the town was recorded in the Domesday Book. In 1086, Grimesbi (as it was spelt) had arable and grazing land as well as a mill and two ferries. Grimesbi built its initial growth on agriculture. It was surrounded on the eastern fringes by marshland, referred as the Fitties, and was not known for the fishing that would later become synonymous with the town.

Grimsby continued to develop during the Middle Ages, and had a fair sized population of 2,000. Its growth, and wealth, is evidenced by the fact that it had two parish churches, St James's, and St Mary's – the latter no longer standing today – and had a nunnery, an Abbey, two friaries, and two hospitals.

In fact much of the medieval street layout can still be seen today, although the only building standing from then is the parish Minster. Parts of that are said to go back to Norman times, and some even suggest that, in places, the brickwork might be Roman.

As the town progressed its fortunes went up and down and it was only the coming of the railways, and the boom in the fishing trade, which seemed to save the town from poverty, and despair. Through reading the many books on the history of the development of the town, it is clear to see that corruption was rife among the Aldermen and Burgesses over the ages.

The town's growth

At the time of the Norman Conquest, Grimsby's land was divided between lords, Odo, the Bishop of Bayeux, Drew De Beurere, and Ralf De Mortemer. Overseas trade and fishing were the mainstay of the town's economy.

As Dowling (2010) tells us, in the latter part of the eighteenth century

Grimsby was merely a market town; it was the actions of some local landowners that made it into the town we know today. The transformation began in 1796 with the creation of the Grimsby Haven Company. The plan was to create a dock, and the money being invested was to come from local farmers, and landowners.

The new dock opened in 1801, and at first it was commercial trade that prospered. It did not last long however, as there was nothing to send back – the trade was only one-way. By the 1840s, due to the lack of trade and merchants, it still was not doing well, despite land on the East Marsh from Pasture Street, up Victoria Street to the docks being sold in lots to create a new town.

Between 1800 and 1832, a total of 573 lots had been created on the East Marsh with roads laid out. Being so close to the dock, the plan had been to provide working class houses. Many of the lots, however, were not built upon but used instead to grow vegetables. From 1827 to 1840, the Enclosures were taking place. This was an Act of Parliament that enclosed open fields and common land creating legal property rights to land that had previously been common. Grimsby's open field system of farming was changing, as fields were enclosed giving rise to smaller fields. By the time the Enclosures were complete, there were just a few

2. Prince Albert opening the Royal Dock.

PRINCE ALBERT'S CARRIAGE DRAWN BY "NAVVIES" TO THE ENTRANCE OF THE DOCK WORKS.

key land-owners: Lord Yarborough, 692 acres; Grimsby Corporation, 538 acres; George Heneage, 160 acres and George Tennyson, 32 acres.

The Municipal Reform Act of 1835 changed the face of local government by taking away ancient privileges and, in effect, cleaning up a political system that had been corrupt for years.

Finally, in 1849 and after many years of conflict over land ownership, the railway to Manchester was opened, followed by a new dock in 1852. It was designed by engineer James Rendel, and officially opened in 1849 by Prince Albert. It was the start of a prosperous time for Grimsby.

Over the following years the docks were extended as the fishing industry boomed. By 1865, Grimsby held the honour of being the fifth largest port in the country and more land was developed as businesses expanded.

However, the people were living in squalor within this 'new town'. The Board of Health inspector reported people living in overcrowded and unhealthy houses with poor sanitation. As the town continued to grow in the 1850s, more housing was needed and the East Marsh and Little Field areas of town were earmarked. Land was sold to raise revenue and the lots were built upon. Grimsby was starting to take shape.

By the 1870s, Freemen Street and the roads branching off it provided houses for fishermen and their families. On the other side of town, Cromwell Road had been built, but the Little Field pastures lay relatively untouched. Around 1873, moves were being made to develop the West Marsh, which until the construction of Corporation Bridge and the Newmarket Street footbridge, had been cut off from the eastern part of town.

The layout of the West Marsh was based on the East, but the Corporation hoped for a better standard of sanitation. When built, the houses were basic working class terraces complete with community

3. Grimsby General Hospital.

THE GRIMSBY & DISTRICT HOSPITAL.

4. Street map of Grimsby, 1893 from an engraving by G Parker.

buildings, plus the town's new hospital was also built here, alongside the River Freshney.

By 1891 the area had been granted county borough status, thanks largely to its MP, Edward Heneage, and so the town we see today was formed.

Landowners

The three prominent families in the town during its growth were the Anderson-Pelhams, who had the title Earl of Yarborough; Heneage, and Grant-Thorold. Others included the Tennyson and Tomline families.

The Tennyson family owned land in the centre of Grimsby. They came to the area in the eighteenth century and married into another prominent family, the Claytons, who had been political giants in the 1790s. When their line died out it was inherited by George Tennyson, and then by his grandson, Frederick, whose brother was the poet laureate, Alfred.

George Tomline of Riby Grove owned land off Cleethorpes Road around the docks. He held the Lincolnshire Militia's honorary title of Colonel, and owned Riby Hall. His family seat, however, was in Suffolk, and he was regarded as the country's second largest landowner.

The Anderson-Pelhams were granted earldom in 1837, thus becoming the Earls of Yarborough. They soon shortened their name to Pelham, and their seat to this day is at Brocklesby Hall. They owned land in the town centre and to the south, comprising of Scartho.

The Grant-Thorolds held lands in Cleethorpes but were key to the development of Grimsby. Their land ran alongside the boundary between East Marsh and Grimsby, and throughout the course of the town's development, this family would have regular feuds with the Heneage family.

The Heneage family, from Hainton Hall near Market Rasen, owned land in Grimsby and Cleethorpes, but had connections with the town going back to the fifteenth century. Heneage imposed high standards for the areas developed, and as Dowling (2010) points out, with the building of different houses for different classes, social engineering was created.

Those living on the Heneage part of town were governed by strict covenants, and there were no public houses. Looking at census returns you can see the rise of people, and their aspirations as they moved from the east area of town to other more affluent parts, such as Abbey Road in Wellow ward.

Street Names of Grimsby

Abbey Drive East/West *see* Abbey Road

Abbey Road

All the Abbey streets – Abbey Park Road, Abbey Drive East/West, Abbot's Way, and Abbey Walk are all connected to the town's former Wellow Abbey. Around the site on which stood the former Abbey, we have Abbey Park Road, which appears in the 1851 Census.

Abbey Road was named in the 1890s, prior to that it was known as Love Lane, and before that Watery Lane. The latter name came from the fact there was a blow well in a field, from which flowed a stream into an open drain on the road.

Wellow Abbey was founded in the time of King Henry I and was a house for the Austinian Canons. It was dedicated to Norwegian

5. Abbey Road also known as Spectacle Row, a modern day view.

6. The former site of Wellow Abbey now occupied by houses.

7. The Abbey, 1860s.

St Olaf and St Augustine – links to the town's Scandinavian origins – and was finally dissolved by King Henry VIII in 1539. In 1911 a seal depicting these saints was found on the Norwegian shore.

Sir Thomas Heneage, who was the last Lord of the Hainton estate, bought the former Abbey land, and a large house was later built on the site before being demolished in 1967. At the time the *Grimsby Evening Telegraph* reported what an outrage it was that the site had not been saved for the town and its people.

Abbot's Way is a relatively new development and one householder, on digging in his garden, did find the grave of a man, believed to have been a monk.

Abbey Park Road *see* Abbey Road

Abbot's Way *see* Abbey Road

Achilles Way

This and other streets on the Laceby Acres are connected with the Battle of Trafalgar – *Achilles* was a 74-gun frigate. Others include Collingwood Way, Hamilton, Africa, Ajax, Belleisle, Brittania, Orion, Sovereign, Swiftsure, Tonnant and Victory Way.

Adam Smith Street

This name recalls Grimsby's rise from obscurity in the eighteenth century to success as a port in the nineteenth, especially from 1850 onwards. Adam Smith was a well-known and respected civil engineer in North Lincolnshire. He was in charge of the Ancholme Navigation improvements and extension and his skill and experience were used in the building of Grimsby Docks.

The street was built in 1882. It runs along the Westgate – A180. The houses have long gone, and it is now part of an industrial estate.

Ainslie Street

Built in 1882, the name commemorates a magnificent benefactor to Grimsby, Canon Robert Ainslie, Vicar of Grimsby (1856–1879). In 1856 the town was developing rapidly and there were no schools for children in a population of 10,000. Canon Ainslie was responsible for the opening of seven new schools. He paid for the cost of two, replaced St James's Church, built St Luke's, St Paul's and St Andrew's, and organised soup kitchens, cheap coal clubs, and other good works. It was only in his later years that Grimsby people began to realise how much he had done for them.

Grimsby author Bob Lincoln wrote:

Ainslie Road then (1882) in the making, was slightly different to the present day. The old White House with the Sand Hills at

8. Old cemetery in Ainslie Street/Doughty Road.

the rear stood where Watson has his dairy, whilst at Isaac Watts' corner, the footpath remained to Old Clee, crossing Legsby Avenue and Hainton St, etc. The remaining route was simply a wilderness. Indeed it was not until some five years after, in 1893, that Messrs. Walker and Cook built the first two houses. They are situated at the corner of Lambert Road, and were occupied by Mr E. R. Wright, the well known school master and Mr Arthur Simons.

The old town's cemetery was opened here in 1859. It closed during the Second World War due to bomb damage and closed officially in 1959 when it was turned into a park.

Airedale

This and Easdale, Farndale, Ravendale, Wharfedale and Whernside, on the West Marsh were created in 1974 by Grimsby Estates Committee. Councillor Peter Ellis had wanted them to commemorate trawler owner, Sir Alec Black, but it was opposed. One councillor did not think the names were fitting for the area but another said people were beginning to think the council were becoming more imaginative with street names.

Albert Street East & West

This street, off Freeman Street, was in existence in 1880 and was probably named in honour of the popular Prince Albert Victor, eldest son of the then Prince of Wales, who became King Edward VII. In 1885

9. Ragged School in Albert Street.

he visited Cleethorpes to open the Pier Gardens, and the Sea Wall built to protect High Cliff. Albert Road and Victor Colonnade in Cleethorpes also commemorate him. There was great national sorrow when he died of pneumonia in 1902. It could also have been named after the Prince Consort, husband of Queen Victoria, who laid the first stone of the Great Grimsby Dock in 1848, and came here again in 1854.

Albion Street

Albion is an ancient name for Great Britain, and is also the name of a former pub on Clee Road. *The Albion* was also a fishing boat sunk off the coast of Spurn Point in July 1918 by a German U-boat.

In 1887 a 24-year-old fisherman called Richard Insole was sent

11. East Marsh flats built in the 1960s - earmarked for demolition in 2016 as part of redevelopment in the area.

10. Albion Street/ Garibaldi Street junction. M. Burton grocers far right. Circa 1950s.

12. Alexandra Dock aerial view.

to the gallows after shooting his estranged wife. The gun used was bought from a gun shop in Albion Street. In 1989, while renovating the Corporation Arms pub in Freeman Street, a notice was found referring to this murder.

Alexandra Road

This highway was named Ropery Lane in a 'Plan of the Town, Harbour and Lordship of Great Grimsby', surveyed by W Smith in 1820. In James Rendel's map of 1848 it was called West Marsh Lane, and in 1905 it was known as Old Dock Road.

Its current name comes from the Alexandra timber dock, which was opened in 1879 by the Prince and Princess of Wales, though it was not given this name until 1913 in honour of the Princess, later Queen Alexandra. The Old Dock, built in 1800, likewise became the Alexandra

Dock. The street was built in 1892. The section between Corporation Road, and the former Adam Smith Street is un-adopted.

Alfred Street

This street runs south from Tennyson Street towards Frederick Street. All these street names commemorate the Lincolnshire Tennyson family, as does Somersby Street. Alfred, its most famous member, was born at Somersby and was Lincolnshire's great poet (1809-1892) and Poet Laureate from 1850 to his death.

By the Grimsby Enclosure Award of 8 May 1840, George Tennyson became the fourth biggest landowner in Grimsby. Charles Tennyson was MP for Grimsby between 1818 and 1820. See also Frederick Street.

Alfred Terrace

Branching off Brighowgate, the current terrace replaced a Georgian one pulled down in the 1980s after having been derelict. It caused outrage in the town at the time. The building was listed, but following a local inquiry, the Secretary of State for the Environment said it was not of any architectural merit and some councillors agreed.

13. Alfred Terrace, 1964. Formerly the House of Industry.

The original was built in 1802 and was a former House of Instruction, in other words, a workhouse and then it was rebuilt in 1850 as private houses.

Algernon Street

Sited in an area of the town once owned by the Heneage Estate and whose family the streets are named after. Sir Algernon Charles Fieschi Heneage was cousin to Edward Heneage, who was MP for Grimsby from 1880.

Sir Algernon entered the navy in 1846 and rose to Admiral. He retired from service in 1898. Sir Algernon died in 1915.

Allestree Drive and Dovedale Drive

The houses in these two streets were built by the well-known Scartho firm, E S Rudkin & Co, which still exists today and were named by the late Mr Rudkin after the Derbyshire scenery.

Anderson Street

Anderson was the family name of the Earls of Yarborough in the eighteenth Century. Mary Pelham, daughter of Sir William Pelham and heiress of Brocklesby, married Francis Anderson in 1708. Their grandson Charles Anderson took the additional name of Pelham on succeeding his great uncle to the title and was created Baron Yarborough in 1794. From then on all future family members used the surname, Anderson-Pelham.

Antrim Way

This along with Lisburn Grove and Ulster Avenue are the Irish connection to the Pelham family title of Fauconberg and Conyers (see Conyers Avenue). Lisburn is a city in the county of Antrim in Ulster (Northern Ireland) while Ulster is one of the four provinces of Ireland.

Annesley Street

This highway has virtually disappeared. It got its name from a former MP for Grimsby, Earl Annesley. He was elected in 1852 with 847 votes, as against 286 for his opponent Edward Heneage. The Earl was described as a 'Liberal Conservative opposed to the Yarborough

14. Arlington Street, off Victor Street, May 1965.

Heneage faction'. The street was built in 1882 and runs off Adam Smith Street on the dockside of the town.

Arlington Street (Lost) *see* Grafton Street

Armstrong Street

Named after Sir William Armstrong, who along with Adam Smith and James Rendel, were mainly responsible for the construction of the Royal Dock. Edward H Clark, in a lecture given to the Institute of Civil Engineers on 29 November 1864, said 'the whole of the machinery, including rollers and paths, was supplied by Sir W Armstrong, and was the first apparatus of the kind designed by him for the purpose of working dock-gates.'

Arthur Street

C H Lingard writing in the local press on 10 October 1930 stated, 'in the Cow Close many are the Christian names of town councillors of the times'. One was Arthur Connell, who entered the Town Council in 1886. By 1910 he had served twelve and a half years on the Council and was also a magistrate. In 1903, an Arthur William Simons was a councillor for the South West Ward and between 1908-13, an Arthur Cook was Chairman of the Pastures Committee.

Arthur Street runs between Lister Street and Haven Avenue, cutting across Lord Street.

Ash Avenue

A cluster of streets off Cross Coates Road named after trees. Others include Birch Avenue, Elm Avenue and Baytree Avenue.

Auckland Road

This road on the dock gets its name from the 4th Lord Auckland (formerly the Hon. William George Eden), chairman of the South Yorkshire Railway when it was taken over by the Manchester, Sheffield & Lincolnshire Railway Company in July 1873. Auckland was a director of the MS & L Railway Co. from 1863 to 1884 and served as Deputy Chairman from 1884 until his death on 27 February 1890.

Augusta Street

Under construction in 1882, it was named after Lady Gertrude Augusta Anderson-Pelham, born in 1861 and sister of the 4th Earl of Yarborough. *15. Augusta Street Barracks.* She married Sir Frank Astley-Corbett, Baronet, of Elsham Hall on 5 June 1882. She died aged 59 in 1920. Branching off this main thoroughfare are Augusta Close and Augusta Oaks.

Ayscough Street

It formerly ran from Adam Smith Street to Oliver Street, crossing Armstrong Street and Corporation Road.

Sir Christopher Ayscough was Mayor of Grimsby in 1511. In 1532 he was summoned 'for converting to his own use a sturgeon.' Sir Edward Ayscough was MP for Grimsby several times between 1685 and 1699, while Ayscoughe Boucherett was Grimsby's MP in 1796, 1802 and 1803.

The most famous Ayscough was Anne, who married Thomas Kyme at Smithfield in 1546, a martyr to the faith, after suffering dreadful tortures and imprisonment in South Kyme Tower.

Stallingborough Church contains several memorials to the Ayscoughs, who linked up with the Heneage family when Anne Ayscough's father married Katherine Heneage as his second wife.

Bargate /Bargate Avenue/Bargate Court

This road is one of the town's ancient thoroughfares, arriving from the south. Its Scandinavian name – *Barre/gata* – suggests a street with a bar. In the Middle Ages the merchants came to sell their wares in Grimsby's

16. St James Terrace, Bargate. Dr Moody's house is on the corner. Moody Lane in the town was named after him. No date given.

17. Bargate Terrace.

market and would have approached from the direction of Scartho or Laceby, up this highway.

According to Gillett (1970), the ancient custom of erecting the bar across the street was resurrected in 1476 to stop merchants' carts from entering the town and damaging the roads and pavements. The bar was believed to have been near to the present day Bargate and Brighowgate junction.

18. Fryston House.

The toll-gate set up in 1765 across the Weelsby Road end was taken down in 1856. Further down Bargate on the left stood the old Wheatsheaf public house, which was one of the outlying buildings of the town until just after the First World War. The old Bargate Cottages still stand near the present site of the Wheatsheaf, which at one time was a girls' school.

At the junction with Welholme Road there once stood an old post windmill, which burned down in about 1847. At the junction of Bargate and Brighowgate was a pinfold where stray cattle were confined until their owners paid a fine to get them out a blue stone stood at the junction of Bargate and Abbey Road to mark the boundary.

Developments began along this road in the 1870s, when people who had made their money in the town began to build large residences as a showcase.

One such residence, Fryston House, which stands on the main junction of Bargate and Weelsby Road, was built in 1875 by grain merchant Robert Norfolk. On the opposite side stands Nunsfield, built in 1890 and occupied for generations by the Mountain family, who set up a firm of solicitors in the town.

Barry Avenue

This road can be found on the south side of Laceby Road. It is said the builder, Ken Sowter, named it after his son. Developed in the 1970s.
Bath Street

This was a sizeable street in 1852 with thirty-one householders. It marked the boundary between Cleethorpes and Grimsby, with a blue stone at the junction of Bath Street and Hope Street. The stone, along with the Havelock stone, which marked the division between Wellow and Grimsby, was to be seen outside the entrance to the Doughty Museum. It's believed its name refers to either a communal bath or a sheep dip.

Baxtergate

This is another of the town's ancient highways. Baxtergate means the 'baker's road', for a Baxter was a 'bakester' or 'baker' derived from the Anglo-Saxon 'bacon' to bake. The Court Rolls for the year 1404 state that one petty constable dealt especially with violence in Baxtergate.

It was re-named Victoria Street when Queen Victoria visited Grimsby in 1854. Before that date, from the Old Market Place to North St Mary's Gate, the road was called Baxtergate West, and from East St Mary's Gate to George Street was Baxtergate East. The name still lives as one of the malls in the shopping centre.

Baytree Avenue *see* Ash Avenue

Beacon Court

On the boundary of Grimsby and Cleethorpes, this road was named after the nearby Beacon Hill.

Beeley Road

Named after the Derbyshire village.

Beeson Street

This was named after the late Alderman Alfred Charles Beeson (1862-1944). Born in Grimsby, he first worked at Smethursts twine spinning and rope merchants, eventually taking over the business and starting up as a painting contractor and paint merchant at Grimsby Docks. In 1910 he was elected councillor for the North East Ward, which he represented until 1926. Elected to the Alderman Bench he served as Chairman of the Corporation Estates Committee for nearly thirty years. He was also Chairman of the Education and Nautical School Committee and was appointed a Justice of the Peace in 1928. He was also President of the Sea Cadet Corps.

Bemrose Way

Named after Grimsby Borough Council's Housing Committee Chairman, Phil Bemrose. Opened in 1980.

Berea, The

This unusual street name was also the name of one of the late Sir Alec Black's trawlers. He planned the streets in this area of town. The houses were built mainly in 1939 and among the builders were Drayton, Dale Bros., H Crampton and Carr for The Berea, The Cresta and Roundway. Some in The Cresta were built in 1945. Berea is also a town outside Durban in South Africa.

Bestall Road

This road is named after one of the town's sporting heroes – Jackie Bestall. He joined Grimsby Town Football Club from Rotherham in 1926, and made 426 appearances for the club, which he captained in the 1930s when it experienced its most successful years.

He played for the Football League and won a full international cap against Ireland in 1935 at the age of 35. He left Grimsby Town in 1938. He was manager of Doncaster Rovers in 1946–7 when the club was promoted to Division Two and also in 1955–6, another promotion year. He was appointed manager for Blackburn Rovers from 1949 to 1953. He was also a very competent cricketer.

20. Yarborough Hotel, Bethlehem Street.

19. Bethlehem Street with Church Lane in the distance and the Yarborough Hotel on the left, circa 1950s.

Bethlehem Street

Known as Bethlem Street on old town maps and named after the Royal Bethel Hospital in London, the world's oldest hospital specialising in mental illness, founded in 1247 by the sisters of the Order of the Star of Bethlehem, after which it was named. The hospital became infamous for its notoriously cruel treatment of patients and, in the eighteenth century, visitors could pay to observe and taunt the patients. Bethlehem Street was also called Low Road in the 1830s.

Standing near the railway station is The Yarborough Hotel, built in 1851 by the second Earl of Yarborough and the Royal Dock Company. In 1862 it was at the centre of a political riot, when John Chapman, chairman of the Manchester, Sheffield & Lincolnshire Railway, was elected MP against George F. Heneage. The election was memorable because the hotel was ransacked and voters were kidnapped, as was often the case in nineteenth century elections led by corruption.

Beverley Crescent

Named after the East Yorkshire town. Other streets in this vicinity of the former Grant-Thorold Weelsby estate are named after Yorkshire and Teesside seaside towns.

21. Duke of York Gardens opening ceremony.

Birch Avenue *see* Ash Avenue

Bishop's Walk

This road along with The Close, Westminster Drive, Canterbury Drive, Tewkesbury Avenue and Malmesbury Drive were named by Edward Heelas, of Grimsby Highways Committee, as appropriate names for streets near St James's School. They maintain the ecclesiastical associations of the district.

Bodiam Way

In the East Marsh, named after the castle in East Sussex. Also close by is Harlech Way, named after the Welsh castle.

Boulevard Avenue

Named after the boulevard created for the town, the Duke of York Gardens. Known by the locals as Bully Avenue it follows the bed of the old Great Coates branch line, which was relocated in 1909 to where it presently runs. This was done as it had cut the Gilbey estate in half, which meant it couldn't be developed. *See* Gilbey Road. The subway was opened in 1941.

Bowers Avenue

The houses here were built by J H Thompson & Sons, Ltd. The street was named after the maiden name of Mr Thompson's mother-in-law.

Bowling Green Lane

James Rendal's map of Grimsby (1848) and another map (1863) show Bowling Green Lane to the south of, and parallel with, Pasture Street. Today it's at right angles to it. In 1848 this lane led off from the south part of Queen Street, which ran across both sides of Pasture Street. The bowling green was situated to the rear of where the Town Hall stands today.

Anderson Bates writing in 1893 about Burgess Street stated 'on the opposite side of the road (i.e. Burgess Street) was a pretty bowling green.'

Bremerhaven Way

Sited on the Bradley Park Estate, it honours Bremerhaven, one of

22. Barclays Bank, Brewery Street.

Grimsby's twin towns in the town-twinning scheme of the 1960s. The estate was developed in 1977.

Bremerhaven is a seaport in Bremen in Germany and is one of that country's most important trading ports.

Brewery Street

There were a number of breweries in the town, Hewitt's Brewery being one of the more significant ones. It ceased trading in 1968 when it was bought out by Bass Charrington. The Hewitt family started the company in the 1870s and from 1890 the family lived at Weelsby Old Hall.

Bridge Gardens

Close to a bridge, which goes over the River Freshney in the West Marsh. Nearby is Haven Gardens, which is connected to the river.

Bridge Street, North and South

The bridge must have crossed over the old Clee Drain, which ran into Boiling House Creek in the first half of the nineteenth century. It is generally agreed the bridge lay between the two Bridge Streets, and that they were named North and South for that reason. But a map of Grimsby

24. Brighowgate.

23. Brighowgate, a sketch by A E Skrill, 1870'

25. The ancient pear tree in Brighowgate.

COLLEGIATE SCHOOL
BRIGHOW GATE. GRIMSBY.

26. Collegiate School, Brighowgate.

dated 1863 shows a bridge crossing the middle of Bridge Street North, which only deepens the mystery.

Brighowgate

Pronounced brigger-gate. This is another of the ancient roads of the old town, and shows its Danish roots. The first part of the name is Scandinavian for a bridge by a spur of land and the latter means road or way. Gate or Gata commonly crops up in the names of the town's streets.

In 1802 the House of Industry, later to become the Workhouse, was sited down here. In Reverend Oliver Wild's *Byrde of Gryme*, he talks of an ancient pear tree, which stood in the grounds of what was formerly the old Grimsby County Court. In the book, he tells the reader the tree was planted in 1484 by Stephen de la See, a rich merchant of the town. It is also alleged that William Shakespeare visited and wrote a sonnet under its branches.

Built in 1902, the old courthouse was designed by the architect Herbert Scaping, well known for having designed many of the town's buildings. The courthouse building is now home to a law firm.

Brocklesby Road/Brocklesby Place

Named after a builder, Mr C Brocklesby, who did much building in that area, east from Little Coates Road in the late 1920s and early 1930s. Also considering the town's connection with the Yarborough family, whose family seat is at Brocklesby, it is quite apt.

Buckfast Way

A series of streets on the Willows Estate all named after abbeys. Buckfast Abbey is found in Devon. The others are Byland Grove, Fountains Avenue, Melrose Way and Tintern Walk.

Buller Street

Named after General Sir Redvers Henry Buller, who commanded the British forces in the Boer War and relieved the township of Ladysmith after several attempts. The street was officially adopted by Grimsby Town Council on 21 July 1902, and the Boer War ended in that same year. See also Durban Road and Ladysmith Road.

Buller led the British troops against the formidable Boers in a number of disastrous battles and was later forced to resign. To some he became a scapegoat for the military, while others believed he had been unfit to serve.

Bull Ring/Bull Ring Lane

Bull baiting took place here until 1779. In the sixteenth century so

27. Bull Ring, circa 1908.

28. Burgess Street, corner with Grimsby Street, 1930s.

much meat theft and black marketing took place in Grimsby, that this 'sport' was approved as one way of keeping a check on it. Court Leaf Records show that Grimsby butchers wishing to kill bulls had first to have them baited by dogs as a public entertainment, which the Mayor and burgesses had to attend.

The Bull Ring was also used for markets and shows. The first non-conformist meeting-house was built there between 1756 and 1759. The famous preacher, John Wesley, who founded Methodism, even preached here. It was also the site of the town's stocks. In 1893 Anderson Bates

29. Lower Burgess Street/Cressey Street junction, circa 1950s. Note the cobblestones and tram lines.

wrote 'I have seen a woman undergoing the degrading punishment of sitting in the stocks.'

During redevelopment of the town the Bull Ring has all but been lost – apart from its name, which is listed above a building in the vicinity of where it stood.

Burgess Street

Named after the burgesses – the Freemen of the town, who had owned vast acres of it since the medieval times. Divided into Upper and Lower. Since the building of the Peaks Parkway, it has been lost in places.

Butchery Lane

Close to the Bull Ring. The site of the butchers', where the bulls were slaughtered after baiting. *See* Bull Ring

Buttermere Way

Named after the Cumbrian lake. Close by are other roads named after Cumbrian places of interest, Millom Way and Seascale Walk.

Cambridge Road

Leading out of the town towards Little Coates. Named after the English university town.

Canterbury Drive

Like other streets in the vicinity, such as Westminster Drive, Bishop's Walk and The Close, they all maintain the ecclesiastical atmosphere and connection with College Street and St James's Church School. See also Malmesbury Avenue and Tewkesbury Avenue.

Carr Lane

In the 1920s, this lane was known as Old Clee Lane. Its name is derived from the word Carr, meaning marshy land in process of being reclaimed. Up until the 1920s–30s, this area of Grimsby was rural. The highway ran over common land in the 1830s.

Cartergate

This is another of the ancient streets of Grimsby. Scandinavian in origin, it was the road used by the merchants to enter the town. Its name

30. Cartergate, looking from Chantry Lane, 1950s.

means the street of the carters and was first recorded in 1406. *See* New Cartergate.

Cartmel Grove

Is named after Cartmel in the Lake District, with which the local building family, Cartledge were associated.

Carnarvon Avenue

One of many streets in this area named after castles and cathedrals. Caernarfon is a North Wales town, home to a spectacular castle.

Carnforth Crescent

Named after the Lancashire town. It was made famous after the railway station was used by David Lean in his film *Brief Encounter*.

Castle Street

In the area of the ducal streets.

Castleford Avenue

Named after the West Yorkshire town.

31. Chantry Lane with a well known shop, Wilson's butchers.

Catherine Street

Named after the youngest daughter of George Robert Heneage, of Hainton Hall. Catherine was sister to Edward Heneage, who was MP for Grimsby in 1880; she married a Major Beresford. Catherine died in 1895.

Cavendish Street

One of the many ducal streets in the town. Lord Cavendish was a friend of Grimsby's MP Edward Heneage.

Central Parade

The main street on the Yarborough estate, renamed recently as Freshney Green.

Chantry Lane

Has historical links going back to 1066 when Raymond the Deacon fought on the Norman side at the Battle of Hastings and was rewarded by grants of land in Grimsby and elsewhere.

In 1314, one of his descendants founded a Chantry – a chapel endowed to support priests to sing masses daily for the deceased. A survey of

Chantry property in the reign of Henry VII (1485-1509) mentions 'two capital messuages, one in Sheyldecroft, another in Chantry Lane'.

An Edmund Grimsby founded a chantry in 1344 in St James Church to pray for his soul and those of his family. This part of the church became known as Rayner Chantry. The priest who looked after this lived in a house which stood in what we know as Chantry Lane.

The present street is relatively modern. Belgrave Terrace in the street was built in 1882.

Chapman Street

Named after John Chapman, who became MP for Grimsby in 1862 defeating George Heneage by 458 votes to 446. In 1865, he lost his seat to John Fildes. *See* Fildes Street.

Charles Avenue

Forming a T-junction with Conyers Avenue, it bears a traditional Christian name in Lord Yarborough's family, as may be seen from a look through Burke's Peerage. The 1897 edition records ten members of the family whose first name was Charles.

Charlton Street

Commemorates Thomas Charlton, Mayor of Grimsby in 1875 and 1876. Known by locals as 'Little Russia', a resident once said this was due to it being an 'overcoat colder' than on the other side of the Cleveland Bridge (a nearby railway bridge).

Chelmsford Avenue

This street is named after the Essex city and is sited on the eastern part of the town. It is linked to Worcester Avenue, which runs parallel to it on the western side of the town, by Eastern Inway and Western Outway. Both avenues are named after cathedral cities.

Chepstow Grove

Named after the Monmouthshire town in Wales, which borders Gloucestershire, England. The town has a castle built in 1067 on the orders of William the Conqueror. Other roads in the vicinity are also named after castles and cathedrals.

Cherry Tree Crescent

This and Laburnum Drive and Maple Avenue are all named after trees.

Chester Grange

Named after Dave Chester, who owned the plot of land where this road and housing estate was built in Scartho. Originally the plot of land had been a smallholding.

Chester Walk

Part of the C-streets. This was named after the Cheshire town lying on the River Dee, near to the border with Wales.

Chestnut Avenue

This was built circa 1907 and so named because four of the front gardens each had a Chestnut tree. At one time this avenue was not listed in any Grimsby street maps. It is found at the end of Wells Street facing the railway.

32. Church Street.

Chingford Avenue *see* Cromer Avenue

Christine Place

Situated in Scartho, this road was named after builder, T W Bygott's daughter Christine. He built the houses in the street.

Church Street

Standing on the corner of this street and Freeman Street, near to Riby Square stood St Andrew's Church, after which the street is named. St Andrew was the patron saint of fishermen. It was demolished in the 1960s to make way for the precinct, though residents were in uproar.

Church View

Located in Little Coates, this road has a view of the nearby church of St Michael's.

Churchill Way

Most likely named after Winston Churchill, prime minister of Great Britain during the Second World War.

Clark Avenue

Like Bowers Avenue, was built in the 1930s by J H Thompson & Sons Ltd. Mr Thompson's wife's maiden name was Clark.

Claremont Road

Named after Claremont House in Surrey. An eighteenth century Palladian mansion once lived in by Thomas Pelham-Holles, the Duke of Newcastle. This road is next to Kelham Road, named after another grand mansion.

Clavering Street *see* Gilbey Road

Clayton Street (Lost)

It lay to the west of Victoria Street and ran parallel to it. Its name commemorates the Clayton family, which dominated Grimsby's trade in the eighteenth century. Christopher Clayton was clerk to the South Sea Company at the start of the century and the family were also engaged in East Indian trade. One Clayton even perished in the

Black Hole of Calcutta, an Indian dungeon in Fort William in Bengal where British prisoners were kept after the Bengali Army captured it in 1756. Towards the end of the seventeenth century the Claytons bought property in Grimsby, especially around the Haven, where they owned a raff-yard (refuse), a brewhouse, brick kilns, and the stone stairs used by inhabitants when taking water from the Haven for brewing.

Christopher Clayton was the first member of the family to become Mayor of Grimsby in 1667. Between 1700 and 1769, the Claytons were Mayors of Grimsby eighteen times. Three Tennysons, William, Ralph and Michael all married into the Clayton family.

Artist George Skelton's drawing shows Clayton Hall in Baxtergate in 1820. Its site was approximately where Argos is today, and it stood in grounds opposite to Osborne Street. Clayton Street was demolished to make way for the shopping precinct.

Cleethorpe Road

This is the main road to the seaside resort of Cleethorpes. Prior to the flyover's erection in the late 1960s, there was a level crossing, which was allegedly one of the busiest in the country as the gates were constantly closed to allow the freight trains carrying fish and coal. It was because of this that it was decided to build a flyover. By the time it was completed however, freight had ceased to be transported this way.

Cobden Street

This street is over 100 years old. A notice in the *Grimsby Observer* of 3 July 1872 states, 'Mr M Wilkin is about to erect 15 tenements in Cobden Street and Holles Street, similar to those already built, at a cost of £120 each.'

It was named after Richard Cobden (1804-65) who, with Bright, led the fight for Free Trade. They travelled all over the UK organising events for the Anti-Corn Law League. Cobden supported temperance, further education, and parliamentary reform. Several streets in Grimsby commemorate radical politicians and authors of the mid-Victorian era.

College Avenue

So called because of its close proximity to St James's College, later St James's School.

Colin Avenue

Houses on this avenue were built by S Cartledge and it was named after his son, Colin.

Columbus Way

Connected to Grimsby's twin town Bremerhaven. Columbus is named after the port's terminal, while nearby Selge Way was named after the Burgomeister and Tallert Way was named after the Oberbürgermeister.

Columbia Road

Probably gets its name from the fact that Colonel Richard Stirling Grant-Thorold at one time owned a ranch in British Columbia. The last peer of Hainton Hall, Reverend Thomas Heneage, was also a rector in British Columbia (1909-12).

Compton Drive

It is said to have got its name because the builder, Mr Drew, was a keen admirer of Denis Compton, cricketer and England football star of the 1930sand '40s. Compton Drive was built in 1935 and adopted in 1939.

33. Convamore Road.

Coningsby Drive

This is named after the Lincolnshire village, which is also home to an RAF base. RAF Coningsby was home to the Dambusters 617 Squadron in the Second World War. Now it is home to the Typhoon and also the Battle of Britain Memorial Flight. Coningsby Drive is one of a number of streets in the vicinity named after Lincolnshire airbases.

Connaught Avenue

Named after ducal titles given to the British Royal Family. Nearby are two other ducal roads, Cumberland Avenue, Devonshire Avenue and Portland Avenue. These regal avenues were planned in the 1900s. Built on land owned by the Heneage estate.

Convamore Road

Named after Convamore Castle in Ireland, the seat of the Earls of Listowel, two miles south east of Castletownrocke in north-east County Cork.

In 1864 Edward, eldest son of George Heneage, married Lady Eleonor Cecilia Hare, youngest daughter of the 2nd Earl of Listowel.

34. Corporation Road bridge opening.

She was sister to Lady Victoria Hare, who in 1858 married the 3rd Earl of Yarborough (see Hare Street).

Heneage was made 1st Baron Heneage on 8 June 1896. Convamore Castle was destroyed by fire in 1921.

Conyers Avenue

This street in Scartho is one of the many Yarborough Estate streets. The 4th Earl of Yarborough married Sophia, Baroness Fauconby and Conyers, on 5th August 1886. The street was adopted on 14 December 1934.

Cooper Road

The first houses here were built in the 1890s by the firm of Cooper and Enderby. It was named after the brother of Mr Cooper's grandfather, who was elected member of the Pastures Committee and of the Freemen's Committee of Auditors for the ensuing year.

Corporation Road

In 1930, C N Lingard, writing in the *Grimsby News* stated, 'In 1865 there was no Corporation Bridge … cowslips grew in abundance where Corporation Road is now.'

After the Grimsby Enclosures of 1827–40, Grimsby Corporation held a considerable area of land in the West Marsh. When the new part of the town in the East Marsh was being built, it was realised that unless a bridge was built across the old dock, Grimbarians would have to walk into the centre of the town in order to reach the West Marsh area. To solve this, the Corporation decided to sell land in the West Marsh to builders and to use the money to build a swing bridge. The bridge was built by Head, Wrightson and Co. of Stockton-on-Tees and opened in 1873.

Corporation Road, formerly a part of West Marsh Lane, was then developed and named after the Corporation. Other streets running off it, or parallel with it, were named mainly after MPs of Grimsby, or people prominent in the development of the Old Dock. Construction on the road began in 1882.

Cotswold Way

Named after the range of hills in western England.

35. Victoria Council School, Cressey Street.

Coventry Avenue

Named after the Midlands town, which is famous for its cathedral, St Michael's which was bombed in the Second World War.

Cragston Avenue

This name has an interesting origin. In the early 1930s, Harry Crompton bought Scartho House and gardens, sited near to the entrance of the Diana Princess of Wales hospital, from Mr Eason. Crompton developed the site and the name Cragston is a combination of his wife's maiden name, Cragg, and the final syllable of his own name – ton.

Crake Avenue

Derives its name from Ernest Edward Crake, Rector of Scartho from 1915 until 1926. He edited *The Parish Registers of Scarthoe, Lincolnshire, 1562-1837* published by Ruddock, Lincoln, in 1926.

Cressey Street

The Cresseys were a prominent Lincolnshire family who had married into the Thorald family at some point in history.

Cresta, The

Like The Berea, this was the name of a trawler owned by Sir Alec Black. *See also* The Berea.

Cromer Avenue

English towns beginning with the letter C, local sources suggest this was probably a deliberate act by the planners. Cromer is a seaside town in Norfolk. Another in the area is Chingford Avenue, which is a suburb of north-east London.

Cromwell Avenue

Houses here were built at the beginning of the twentieth century. In his books, Bob Lincoln tells how, in 1904, he and a Jonathan Markham demolished with axes a palisading erected across the 30ft grass avenue there by 'a certain fish merchant living in the locality'. The fence was re-erected and again demolished. The fish merchant eventually threatened the law. 'I advised him to consult Mr W. G. He did and that staunch advocate of Freeman's rights speedily convinced him that it

36. Anthony Crosland, MP at the announcement of the election result, 31 March 1966. (L-R) Unknown, Anthony Crosland, Dennis Petchell, Fred Ward, Town Clerk and unknown.

was a mistaken policy he had been pursuing.' Cromwell Avenue was built in 1909.

Cromwell Road

Houses here were built in the early 1890s, and it is mentioned in the Grimsby & Cleethorpes Directories of 1893. Though situated in the general area of the former Yarborough Estate, it was not part of it. It is, however, significant that three streets in the area, Cromwell Road, Hume Street and Macauley Street, bear the names of advocates of democratic rule, when one recalls the support given by the Pelham family to the Reform Bill of 1832 and subsequent Acts enlarging the franchise for parliamentary elections. The land for making the road was sold in 1878.

Crosby Road

This could be connected to Henry James Frederick Crosby, a town councillor in 1913. Captain Crosby led the Rifles in the Mafeking Celebrations in Grimsby in 1900.

Crosland Road

Commemorates Charles Anthony Raven Crosland, MP for Grimsby from October 1959 to February 1977, when he died from a heart attack. During the Second World War he served in the Royal Welsh Fusiliers before transferring to the Parachute Regiment in 1942. He was captain in this regiment from 1943 to 1945.

After the war he was Lecturer in Economics at Trinity College, Oxford, from 1947 to 1950, and MP for South Gloucestershire 1950–55. While MP for Grimsby he held the following posts: Minister of State for Economic Affairs, Secretary of State for Education and Science, President of the Board of Trade, Secretary of State for Local Government and Regional Planning, Minister for the Environment, and Foreign Secretary, the last from April 1976.

Cross Street

Found on the docks, it is named after Sir Richard Asheton Cross, MP, who held government office as Home Secretary under Lord Salisbury and was later Secretary of State for India. He was also a director of the Great Central Railway Company. It is said that the Great Central Board meetings were generally dull affairs and that his long whiskers

37. Actress Dame Madge Kendal attending a tea party at Scartho Hospital, 1928.

and picturesque appearance were the only diverting objects When any subject was under discussion, he would murmur as if in his sleep: 'Where is the money to come from?'

Crowland Avenue

Named after the Abbey of Crowland in Lincolnshire. Originally it was an island and in AD 701 a monk called Guthlac lived here as a hermit. Other monks soon joined him and the abbey was constructed. It was finished in 1539 under the Disssolution. The River Welland flows through here. *See* Welland Avenue.

Cumberland Avenue *see* Connaught Avenue

Dame Kendal Grove

Commemorates the famous Victorian actress Dame Madge Kendal who was born at the Railway Tavern, later the Railway Hotel, opposite to the Cleethorpes Road railway crossing, on 15 March 1848.

She was well known in the Victorian and Edwardian eras for her stage performances in Shakespearean and English comedies. Her husband, William Kendal, was also an actor. She was awarded the title of Dame for her services to the acting profession.

In 1928 and 1931 she visited Grimsby to make appeals for the local hospital and donated £500. She was given the Freedom of the Borough on 26 July 1931. She died on 14 September 1935 aged 86 at her Hertfordshire home. A memorial service for her was held at St James's Church, Grimsby, and was attended by the Mayor, council and other officials.

Lincoln (Vol I) says Kendal's parents were performing in the town's first theatre and she was born in the house 'situated at the end of the ropery founded by Captain Harriss, near the far corner of Riby Square.'

38. Deansgate Bridge.

39. Deansgate at the junction with the Bull Ring.

David Street

Built on land belonging to the Heneage Estate. No more is known about who David was.

Davison's Avenue

Is one of Grimsby's mystery streets, as it was not shown in the geographic street plan of the town. It was built in the 1890s by Levi Davison and lies off the bottom end of Frederick Street, to the right, and at one time contained six houses, which faced a piece of unkempt grass. Another approach to it is by going down Alfred Street.

Deansgate

The name is considered by some historians to be a corruption of Danesgate and is taken as further evidence of Grimsby's Scandinavian origin. But it could also be reference to 'The Dean's Road'.

One of the drawings by local artist George Skelton is of the old Deanery in Church Lane. Deansgate is mentioned in the Court Rolls of 1501, when 'the servants of Alexander Del See made two great gifts in the common way against his close in Deansgate for replacing a wall, to the harm of all people coming into the town'.

Deansgate of course, was originally a road over flat land and the bridge and Deansgate Hill were constructed to cross over the railway after 1848.

Devonshire Avenue *see* Connaught Avenue

Dial Square (Lost)

The Square existed in 1826 and by 1852 it had four inhabitants. Artist George Skelton's drawing shows the dial over a building on the north side of the square. In 1913 Bob Lincoln wrote, 'opposite Pailthorpes we find Dial Square. The dial is still to be seen.'

This diamond-shaped dial was eventually replaced by a clock. The dial, bearing the date 1826 and encased in a short brickwork tower was, in the late 1970s, seen in the back garden of a house in Chantry Lane. Dial Square was in the vicinity of the River Head.

Digby Gardens

Another road named after a Lincolnshire village and airbase from the Second World War.

40. George Doughty at the opening of the Strand Street School.

41. Doughty Road plaque when the subway and road was officially opened in 1895 by Sir George Doughty.

42. Diamond Jubilee Homes on Doughty Road.

43. Territorial army marching down Doughty Road.

Dolby Vale

Sited on the Bradley Park estate, it is named after the late Sidney Vere Dolby, a pioneer of radiography who sacrificed his life to help in the healing of others. At the age of 16 he assisted with the building of the first x-ray apparatus at the Grimsby and District General Hospital. In 1910 he performed part time duties as radiographer there and continued his work during the First World War.

Shortly after the Armistice he joined the hospital's full time staff. Over the course of Dolby's career, repeated exposure to radiation led to the loss of his right arm and the three middle fingers of his left hand.

44. TA barracks gate, which stood on Doughty Road.

From 1937 he was continuously under treatment until his death on 16 March 1947 at the age of 61 years.

Donnington Street

Named after a Lincolnshire village in the area of the Hainton estate owned by the Heneage family.

Doughty Road

Named after George Doughty, twice Mayor of Grimsby and knighted in 1904. He was MP for the town in 1895, and again in 1910. He was a merchant and ship owner, and died in 1914.

As Alderman Doughty he officially opened the subway to replace the Peppercorn Walk crossing in 1895. The road was named in his honour. The project cost £7,000. Doughty was Chairman of the Highways and Public Works Committee at the time.

45. Central Hall, Duncombe Street.

46. Duncombe Street terraces.

Drew Avenue

Built in the late 1930s it was named by the Town Council after Mr Cecil Drew, who built the road and houses and laid the drains.

Duchess Street

Could be part of the ducal streets (See Duke Street, Wellington Street).

Dudley Street

Was built in 1882 and named after Dudley Pelham, born 1872, the 4th Earl of Yarborough's brother. Dudley was a captain in the 10th Hussars and served in the Boer War. He was captured at Sanna's Post and became a prisoner of war for several months. In 1938 he was the High Sheriff of Lincolnshire. He died in 1953.

Duke Street

Was constructed in 1882 in the same year as Grafton Street, in the area named after ducal estates. Could also be reference to Arthur Wellesley, 1st Duke of Wellington (*see* Wellington Street).

Duncombe Street

This name is another echo from Grimsby's political past. Before the passing of the Reform Bill in 1832, Grimsby returned two members to parliament. In 1820 two Tory candidates were elected, Charles Tennyson with 227 votes and William Duncombe with 204. Duncombe was elected MP for Grimsby from 1820 to 1825.

Dunmow Street *see* Gilbey Road

Durban Road

Named after the Natal city. It is one of many streets in this area of town to have connections with the Boer War. See Buller Street and Ladysmith Road.

Durham Avenue

Named after the cathedral city of Durham in the north east of England. Durham Cathedral was built in 1093 and is renowned for its magnificent Romanesque architecture. The city lies on the River Wear. The cathedral and the castle were designated World Heritage Sites in 1986.

47. Hewitt's Brewery, East Street.

48. East Marsh Street subway.

Earl Street

Refers to the Earl of Yarborough and is part of the Yarborough Estate. For years it linked up with Yarborough Street, but it did not do so before 1884. In that year the Town Council 'discussed the building of the bridge over the River Freshney connecting Earl Street with Yarborough Street and affording better access to South Parade School for the children in the Cow Close district'. The estimated cost to the Corporation was £400 and the Earl of Yarborough agreed to pay the remainder of the cost of building the bridge.

East End Close

This street in Scartho is so named as it is located on the east side. The road was built on what was formerly Pennells nursery. Hark back to the Enclosures Act as the East End Closes were listed.

East Street/Eastgate (Lost)

Sited on the east side of town. Former site of Hewitt's Brewery.

East Marsh Street

Up to the end of the eighteenth century, Grimsby was bounded by the Haven, which was crossed by a wooden bridge into an open marsh, the East Marsh. This suffered from the effects of tidal waves and there were no houses there. As the Haven silted up the East Marsh area grew larger and became the chief common for grazing.

It was used by the Borough Freemen, but after the building of the Old Dock in 1800, more and more building plots were granted in the East Marsh.

A foot subway was built in 1904 and 61 East Marsh Street, which was beyond the subway, was noteworthy as dating from the early nineteenth century and had a conservation order on it. It was the property of the British Railway. According to some, there was in the yard at the side of it, a furnace where the carcases of horses were burned. The house, one part of which was used as offices, had been a stately home reminiscent of nearby Bennett's Hall, now gone, as is number 61.

Only a fragment of East Marsh Street remains today, sited behind the Asda supermarket.

49. Edward Street School.

Eastwood Avenue

Named after John Basil Eastwood, whom Eleanor Heneage married. She was the daughter of Edward Heneage, MP for Grimsby, who owned the land. This and Portland Avenue were planned in 1914. At the end of this Avenue is sited the cenotaph. At one time this area was the site of the gallows. *See* Nuns' Corner.

Edge Avenue

This road in Scartho was built as part of the 1950s development phase.

Edmonds Way

Situated on the West Marsh, it was named after Ray Edmonds, twice winner of the World Amateur Snooker Championship and a former English professional billiard player. He set up a snooker centre in the town in 1983. He was a snooker commentator for both ITV and the BBC before retiring in 2004.

The street name was proposed by Councillor Alf Chatteris and agreed by Grimsby Housing Committee on 13 January 1975.

The street was first named Easdale Way, but this caused some letters to be sent to Eskdale Way on the Willows Estate and vice-versa.

Edward Street

Son of George Fieschi Heneage, Edward was MP for Lincoln from 1865 to 1868 and then Grimsby in 1880, but lost that seat in 1882. He married Eleanor Cecilia, daughter of William Hare, 2nd Earl of Listowel in 1864. Eleanor Street is named after her (see Hare Street).

The couple had three sons and six daughters. He died aged 82 in 1922 and was succeeded by his son, Lieutenant Colonel George Heneage (1866-1954). In his time he gave People's Park to the people of Grimsby (see Park Avenue).

Eleanor Street *see* Edward Street

Named after the local MP Edward Heneage's wife, Eleanor. She was the daughter of the 2nd Earl of Listowel. She was a renowned horsewoman. Her eldest daughter was also called Eleanor and she married Basil Eastwood (see Eastwood Avenue).

In an article in the *Grimsby News* of 1949, it states that residents are used to windowsills dropping, or doors twisting, because the houses were built on a tidal creek, which ran underground from Bargate.

Elm Avenue *see* Ash Avenue

Escart Avenue

Built by S Cartledge & Son Ltd and so named after the company – S Cart.

50. Corby House on Wellowgate, home to architect Ernest Farebrother and his actress daughter, Violet.

Ethelstone Road and Fannystone Road

Houses here were built by a Mr Fox and the streets were named after his wife and mother. It seems there was some controversy among the Town Council before the names were finally approved. The road was adopted in 1933.

Evelyn Grove

Received its name from Evelyn Hammond, daughter of the builder, Sam Cartledge.

Farebrother Street

Commemorates Violet Farebrother, the celebrated Grimsby born actress of stage, film and television, and her father, Ernest, who died when she was 3 years old. He designed the workhouse in 1890 as architect to the Board of Guardians. He was a well-known architect who designed Corby House in Wellowgate, where Violet was born, and the old Prince of Wales Theatre in Freeman Street. After his death, Violet went to live with her uncle, Tom Sutcliffe, at Stallingborough Manor (*See* Sutcliffe Avenue).

She made her first stage appearance at The Duke of York's Theatre, London, in 1907 and appeared at Grimsby Prince Of Wales Theatre in 1909 with the Benson Shakespeare Company; again in 1921 and in 1923 in *The Borderer*. In 1951 she was a Patron of Grimsby's Caxton Players. She died aged 81 at Eastbourne.

Faringdon Road *see* Henderson Street

Fauconberg Avenue

This road in Scartho was named after the wife

51. John Fildes, MP for Grimsby, 1865

52. Fish Dock Road.

of the 4th Earl of Yarborough, who married Baroness Fauconberg and Conyers on 5th August 1886. It is one of many streets in Scartho and Grimsby to be named after members of the Yarborough family, as he is a significant landowner here. *See* Conyers Avenue.

Ferriby Lane

By the award of the Enclosure of Scartho, 1795–98, lands, where Ferriby Lane stands now, were granted to an Elizabeth Ferriby, whom the lane is named after. At the time of the development of Scartho Top in the early twentieth century, Ferriby Lane was sealed off at the Scartho Road end and access is now gained through Pelham Avenue.

Fildes Street

This was named after one of the town's MPs, John Fildes, who defeated John Chapman (*see* Chapman Street) in the 1865 Parliamentary Election. He was also a director of the Manchester Sheffield & Lincolnshire Railway Company. The street was built in 1882.

53. Flottergate showing the chapel and the Ship Inn.

54. The Black Swan, known as The Mucky Duck, it stood on Flottergate, and was said to have been one of the oldest pubs in Grimsby. Stood where the southwest entrance to Freshney Place is.

Filey Road

Part of a cluster of roads on the former Weelsby estate owned by Grant-Thorold, which are named after seaside villages in Yorkshire and Teesside. Others include Saltburn Grove, Seamer Grove, Whitby, Redcar Grove, Bempton Road and Carnaby Grove.

Fish Dock Road

This street is self-explanatory as it is named after the fish docks.

Fiskerton Close

This street was named after the Lincolnshire village near Lincoln. It was also an airfield in the Second World War and was home to Lancasters from 49 and 576 Squadrons. *See* Goxhill Gardens and Wickenby Close.

Florence Street

Named after Edward Heneage's third child, the Hon. Florence Cecilia, born in 1869.

Flottergate (Lost)

No longer physically in existence, its name still exists within the Freshney Place Shopping precinct. Flottergate ran from Victoria Street (where the entrance to the current shopping centre and market is) to Alexandra Road. This is another of the town's ancient roads and was at one time called Queen Street, after the first Queen Elizabeth. Flotter comes from the Middle English 'floter' meaning to float or flutter and gata, as we know means a street in Scandinavian. It first appears in town records in 1366.

Many older residents will recall The Black Swan (aka Mucky Duck), which stood at the top of Flottergate. Built circa 1699, it was said to have been one of the oldest houses in Grimsby before demolition in 1925 and was replaced by another public house bearing the same name, before it too was demolished in 1971.

In the 1826 Lincolnshire Directory it is listed as Fluttergate. According to Frank Walsham's article in the *Grimsby News* in 1969, it means the road of the stream, as the Haven would flood and flow down the road.

Flour Square

Originally named Flower Square, it had a name change in the 1940s as it was in the vicinity of the Victoria Flour Mill near to the docks. Its original name Flower was believed to have been a mis-spelling of flour.

Fotherby Street

Though a village between Grimsby and Louth, it could commemorate Grimsby-born Dr John Fotherby, who was once Dean of Canterbury in the 1600s. He left in his will in 1619 an annuity of £4 to be paid for a sermon and the rest for the poor. It was known as 'Fotherby's Dole'. The family were an ancient Grimsby family and great benefactors to what is now St James's Minster. According to Oliver (1866) the family rebuilt the chancel after the Reformation and it was known as Fotherby's aisle.

Most of this area of town was demolished after the Second World War and is now home to different industries. Standing at the junction of this street with King Edward Street is St Barnabas Church, though now home to a removals company.

Fraser Street

Georgina Mary, sister of Edward Heneage, married the Hon. Alexander Fraser, second son of the 12th Lord Lovat.

Frederick Street

Named after Frederick Tennyson (1807-1898), second son of Dr George Clayton Tennyson, Rector of Somersby, and elder brother of Alfred, Lord Tennyson. Frederick was also a poet. Four lyrics by him can be found in Palgrave's second *Golden Treasury*.

Born at Louth on 5 June 1807, he was educated at Eton, where he was Captain of the School

55. Prince of Wales Theatre, Freeman Street.

St. Andrew's Church, Grimsby.

56. St Andrew's Church, corner of Freeman Street and Church Street.

57. Freeman Street Market circa 1900s.

in 1827. In 1832 he graduated as Bachelor of Arts of Trinity College, Cambridge. He travelled in Europe and lived in Florence for twenty years. In 1839 he married Maria Giuliotti. In 1841 he moved to St Ewald's, Jersey, then later to Kensington where he died on 26 February 1898.

58. River Freshney.

Frederick Ward Way

Named after Frederick William Ward, clerk to the council. He was made High Steward of the Borough of Grimsby in 1986. The road was opened on 14 June 1988. It runs along the river through what was the medieval port of Grimsby.

Freeman Street

Named in honour of the Freemen of Grimsby in 1859. They owned most of the land in the borough. This was one of the first streets to be built and occupied on the East Marsh along with Kent Street.

The design and layout of the East Marsh estate was prepared by Messrs. Maughan and Fowler, Louth in 1857. There was much demand for plots of land.

Freeman Street Market officially opened in 1873 and still exists today, having undergone some changes. One of the famous eating

59. Garden Street and the junction with South St Mary's Gate with George Capes standing in front of his father's grocer shop 1891.

60. Garden Street, showing Axel Terrace and Graham Terrace.

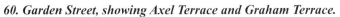

establishments in the area is of course the Pea Bung, started in 1883 by Sally Cox. It is said to be the town's oldest restaurant.

The street was the main thoroughfare to the newly built docks. Sadly now the street has declined and many shops are empty. There is talk of parts of it being demolished and rebuilt, while other areas will be renovated.

Freshney (Street) Drive

Named after the River Freshney, which is in the vicinity. Renamed 'Drive' along with Yarborough Drive in 1974 after residents complained about the stigma of the old area.

Frusher Avenue

Named by Edmund Marshall after his wife's grandfather.

Fryston Corner

Named after Fryston House standing on the corner and built in 1875 by grain merchant, Robert Norfolk. Originally the house was called Southfield.

Garden Street

Writing about this street in 1930, C. H. Lingard in the Grimsby News stated 'up to some forty years ago were a number of old

61. Garibaldi Street Chapel.

thatched cottages on the west side and on the east side nothing but a garden. Formerly known as Gardener's Lane, it reached Abbey Road near the end of what is now Duchess Street.'

At that time there were no buildings in it over the railway crossing, which was practically only used as the nearest way to the Old Cemetery in Ainslie Street.

The street consisted of terraces – King Terrace, Amelia Terrace, Jasper Terrace, Axel Terrace, Cassandra Terrace, Railway Terrace and Abbey Cottages.

In the *Grimsby Observer* in 1885, it was noted that a young child called Albert Stanley had been killed after his head was crushed at the Garden Street railway gates.

According to Cameron (1997), the former name Gardener's Lane was named after the family of an Ambrose Gardiner. In the *Grimsby Evening Telegraph* of 1941, it says there was an orchard, which ran to the railway and the street was named so.

Garibaldi Street

Why should a Grimsby street be named after an Italian soldier and patriot? The answer is that in the decade 1860–70, Great Britain was enthusiastically supporting the movement for the unification of Italy led by Garibaldi, Cavour and Mazzini.

Garibaldi was the hero of the working classes for promoting universal suffrage and supporting the women's movement.

Garner Street

62. George Street Chapel.

The only connection found was that there was a Garner family who were connected to the town. They had connections with the builder G. H. Hipkin and at one time E. Garner was a director of the Grimsby Fish Meal Company.

Garth Lane

This was originally called Colegarths, because Grimsby ship owners imported coal from Newcastle-upon-Tyne and unloaded it there. In his '*History of Grimsby*', the Reverend M. Davies states that the Grey Friars had a house in Garth Lane, 'so as to be in touch with the sailors and port' and that the house was bought by John Kingston, grandfather of Gervase Holles, who stated that he himself was born there and lived there till 1617. Edward Gillett, however, declares that the site of the Grey Friars was near the present Friargate crossing. Part of the medieval port of Grimsby.

Gate Lane

Sited in Scartho, it marks the place where one of the tall gates was situated on the turnpike road to Louth. Greenwood's Map of Lincolnshire shows it and the other turnpike roads and gates.

George Street

Reference to George Fieschi Heneage (1800-1864) who was once High Sheriff of Lincolnshire and MP for Lincoln, but never Grimsby. He was the father of Edward, MP for Grimsby.

Gertrude Street

On land belonging to the Heneage estate. This road was named after Edward Heneage's daughter, Gertrude Mary, born in 1881. She died aged 46 in 1927 having never married.

Gilbey Road

Named after the Gilbey family from Bishop's Stortford, Hertfordshire.

63. Dixons Paper Mill, Gilbey Road.

Sir Walter Gilbey purchased a majority of the Little Coates parish in 1898.

He was originally from a farming family, but had made his money in the import of wine. The business flourished and Gilbey had soon created a nationwide chain of agents selling a range of wine and spirits. He also set up a gin distillery. He received his baronetcy in 1893.

The newly bought land on the West Marsh was initially cut off from the railway, which ran down what is now Boulevard Avenue. In 1901 the railway company re-routed the line, opening the land for further development.

In 1909 the Gilbey Road Board School was opened. Sir Walter died in 1914.

Hargrave Street and Stansted Street were named after Gilbey's house, Hargrave House in Stansted, Hersfordshire, while Clavering Street was named after the village of the same name near Stansted. Nearby Harlow Street was named after the location of Gilbey's gin distillery. Elsenham Road was named after the location of his estate, Elsenham Hall, where he lived from 1874. Dunmow Road was a village near to Bishop's Stortford and Stortford Street was named after his former home town.

Harlech Way *see* Bodiam Way

Glebe Road

Situated in Scartho, gets confused with the street of the same name in Humberston. Sited on former church land, hence the word Glebe. Started out as a cinder track leading to a farmhouse and farm cottages, which still stand. In 1964 the road was finally tarmacked after the residents paid for it themselves.

Gloucester Avenue

Another of the cathedral roads in this vicinity of the town. Gloucester cathedral started out as a monastery and grew to become an important religious house, which saw the crowning of King Henry III in 1216.

Gorton Street

This is named after Gorton Station near Manchester, opened 23 May 1842 as part of the Sheffield, Bolton-under-Lyne and Manchester Railway. In 1845 a project was started for the building of a locomotive and carriage works there. In 1855 a school was built there for the children of company employees, plus a dining room, library, and reading room for adult workers. In 1858 it produced its first locomotive. The works were steadily developed and extended by the Manchester Sheffield & Lincolnshire and Great Central companies. By 1865 replacing, rebuilding and constructing of new locomotives was being undertaken and the works later included locomotive sheds, carriage and wagon shops, and staff cottages.

64. Grant Thorold Park opening.

Goxhill Gardens

Part of a number of streets named after Second World War airbases. Goxhill, which is a Lincolnshire village, was also an airbase for the United States Army Airforce 8th Air Force. The 8th used it as a training base for the Fighter Group. It is rumoured that Hollywood heartthrob Clark Gable trained here.

Grafton Street

Has   a

65. St Giles monument to those killed in the Scartho zeppelin raid by John Grantham, whom Grantham Avenue is named after.

link with Grimsby's political past. In the 1830 parliamentary election, Captain George Harris, a Tory, and Charles Wood, a Whig, were relieved as Grimsby's MPs. In 1831, on 2 May, Harris was again returned with John Villiers Shelley, another Tory. But after a petition, the election was declared void and another one held, at which the Hon. Henry Fitzroy was successful. The Duke of Grafton was his uncle. The street name links up with other 'ducal' streets in the neighbourhood such as Hamilton and Rutland Streets.

Grafton Street has a link with Arlington Street and Duke Street. Henry Charles Fitzroy was created first Duke of Grafton in 1675. In 1682 aged 9, he married 5-year-old Isabella, in her own right Countess of Arlington, who in 1672 had succeeded her father, Henry Bennet, who had been created Baron Arlington of Arlington.

Grant Street

Helen Thorold married Alexander Grant of London, whom the road is named after. The family later changed their name to Grant-Thorold.

Grantham Avenue

Commemorates a generous public benefactor of Scartho, John Grantham. He presented the tower clock in St Giles Church and the monument in the churchyard marking the spot where a bomb fell during a German air-raid in 1916. In the avenue are six almshouses. John Grantham left a trust for these for parishioners of Scartho and Bradley.

Granville Street

Named after Lieutenant Colonel The Hon. Henry Granville Heneage, second eldest son of the town's MP Edward Heneage. Interestingly, he shares a name with his first cousin on his mother's side, the Hon. Richard Granville Hare, who became the 4th Earl of Listowel.

Greethams Lane

This lane in Old Clee is presumably named after the Greetham family, who may have given their name to it. The family are listed as having been here for generations.

Grime Street

Believed to have been named after the family of Walter Gryme from the

66. Hainton Avenue, after the tree planting on the suggestion of the residents.

thirteenth century Grimsby Court Rolls. Gryme is probably a hark back to the town's name of Grim.

Grosvenor Street

This highway runs between Brighowgate and the Bargate/Deansgate junction where a majority of the streets are named after members of

67. Hainton Street.

68. Welhome Congregational Church, Hainton Avenue.

the Earl of Yarborough's family. When this street was constructed in the 1880s, there was a crooked footpath here called Shag-foal Lane. A shag-foal was the name given to a hairy foal, but was also a nightly phantom. The street was developed around 1889. In the *Grimsby News* of 14 June 1889 it was reported that the Duke of Portland married Miss Dallas-Yorke in which the Bishop of Lincoln officiated and the wedding buffet was held at 17 Grosvenor Street, London. Most likely named in

69. Hamilton Street, August 1971.

homage to Grosvenor Square in London, which was a place of high society. Grimsby's namesake was in a well-to-do area of the town and the grandeur of the name would reflect this. Grosvenor is the family name of the Dukes of Westminster.

Guildford Street

In the twenty-first century, this street was to be the source of much anger as residents were moved out and the Victorian houses demolished. It was named after Hilda Grant-Thorold's residence. She married Lieutenant Colonel Augustus Campbell Spencer and they lived at Pattenham, near Guildford in Surrey, which is the origin of the street's name. *See* Hilda Street.

Hainton Avenue/Hainton Square

Named after Hainton Hall the Lincolnshire estate of the Heneage family, who owned the land in this area of Grimsby. Originally called Street, it was renamed Avenue around 1889 after residents proposed the change when trees were planted.

Hamilton Street

Alexander William Thorold Grant-Thorold married Anne Hamilton, daughter of Admiral Sir James Stirling, in 1863. Grant-Thorold (1820-1908) had five children: Richard Stirling, Harry, Frank Hamilton, Hilda, and Constance Mary.

His granddaughter Bridget Mary, the eldest daughter of Harry Grant-Thorold, maintained this street-name link by marrying Lieutenant Colonel T. F. C. Hamilton, OBE, MC in 1945.

70. Municipal College on Harold St.

Hare Street

Named after the father of Lady Victoria Alexandrina Hare, wife of the

71. Haven Street, believed to be from the 1960s.

3rd Earl of Yarborough, and Lady Eleanor Cecilia Hare, wife of Edward Heneage. Their father was William Hare, 2nd Earl of Listowel.

Hargrave Street *see* Gilbey Road

Harlow Street *see* Gilbey Road

Harrison Street

Named after Alderman Harrison Mudd, who entered the council in 1874 and was elected Alderman in 1889. He was Mayor of Grimsby 1900 01 and was still on the Alderman's bench in 1909. The name also commemorates Henry Harrison (*see* Henry Street).

Harold Street

On 30 June 1904, Grant Thorold Park was opened by Captain Harry Grant-Thorold, as the family had given nine acres for its construction. In a dispute over access to the East Marsh years previously, neighbouring landowner, Lord Heneage, had said that Thorold had to devote twenty

72. Summerhouse on Haven Street.

acres of his estate to a playing area. This street is named after his (Harry's) full Christian name, Harold.

73. Holme Hill School on Heneage Road.

Havelock Street (Lost)

In honour of Prince Havelok, from the town's myth. Fisherman Grim was said to have rescued the young Havelok from near death and brought him to Grimsby in his fishing boat. Later in life the prince married Goldborough and Grim founded the town and lived in a house constructed from a boat. The street was demolished in the 1950s.

Haven Street

It appears on James Hollinsworth's plan of Great Grimsby in 1801. In 1852 it had eleven householders plus the Custom House. In the Middle Ages, the west side of the Haven was the trading section of the port and the most important merchants lived in the street. In the 1850s the street housed such well known citizens as Charles Surfleet, Robert Blew, a Mr Screw JP, and Henry Tritton, Customs Officer.

Haycroft Avenue

This avenue runs from Haven Avenue to Cromwell Road and has a subway under the railway near Lincoln Boulevard. For years, that part of it on the Cromwell Road side of the subway had no name sign.

The Haycroft was part of the town's open field system, which existed until 1827. It lay north of the Little Field and reached the boundary with Little Coates. It had an area of fifty-nine acres.

Heneage Road

Named after the Heneage family of Hainton Hall, who owned lands in this area of town and who had connections going back to 1545. George Fieschi Heneage, born in 1800 was MP for Grimsby and Lincoln for seventeen years. He was also High Sheriff of Lincolnshire in 1839.

The streets in this area are named after his family and the estate. Heneage married Frances, daughter of Michael Tasburgh, whom Tasburgh Street is named after. Their son Edward Heneage was a politician.

Henderson Street

This was named after Alexander Henderson, a financier and, from 1899, the chairman of the Great Central Railway Company. In 1894 he raised capital for the Manchester Sheffield & Lincolnshire Railway Company's extension to London. In 1896 he and Pollitt formed the

Wharncliffe Dwelling Company to accommodate the 3,073 inhabitants of the 507 houses demolished as the result of this extension. They built six blocks of five-storied buildings in Wharncliffe Gardens.

Henderson also became a director of the Manchester Sheffield & Lincolnshire Railway Company from 1894 to 1899.

As Sir Alexander Henderson he, along with Sir George Doughty and the Earl of Yarborough, were members of a deputation to the Board of Trade to build a new dock at Immingham, which was formally opened by King George V on 22 July 1912. He helped to promote the building of Fish Dock No 3, which was delayed by the First World War until 1934. He was elevated to the peerage as Lord Faringdon in 1916 and was Deputy Chairman of the London North Eastern Railway.

Hereford Avenue

Another cathedral road. Named after Hereford cathedral rebuilt around AD 1020 by Bishop Athelstan. *See* Gloucester Avenue and Worcester Avenue.

Henry Street

This is a 'Councillor' Street in the Cow Close (Macauley Street) area of Grimsby. Henry Harrison entered the Town Council in 1891 and was elected Alderman in 1910. By 1915 he had served twenty-three years on the council. Another, Henry Smethurst, was elected Alderman in 1889, and was still on the council in 1914. By June 1913 he had sat 'continually on the council for 40 years'.

Heron Close

Houses here were built by Dale and Bromley, of Cleethorpes. It obtained its name from the fact that St Andrew's Steam Fishing Company's telegraphic address was Heron, Hull.

Highfield Avenue

This area was developed in 1909 and was part of Heneage's Highfield Farm estate, which lay off Park Avenue. Bob Lincoln mentions it among 'the large quantity of undedicated streets laid out as grass lanes with footpaths on one side'. Others mentioned by him are Cromwell Avenue, New Bridge Terrace (between Deansgate and Cartergate, the new bridge being Deansgate Bridge), Peaksfield Avenue (Peaks Lane,

Peak's Avenue and Peak's Farm are all from the Peaks family's lands), Princess Avenue, Queens Parade and West Parade, 'the whole of which are fully developed except Cromwell Avenue'.

Hilary Road

This Scartho street received its name in 1930 and replaced the rather quaint name of Red Apple Gardens. Unfortunately, there is no record as to who Hilary was.

Hilda Street

Hilda, the daughter of Alexander Grant-Thorold, married a member of the Spencer family and lived at Pattenham, near Guildford in Surrey. She married Lieutenant Colonel Augustus Campbell Spencer, late 5th Lancers and 1st Dragoon Guards on 12 October 1886. She died 10 July 1952 (*see* Spencer Street).

Hildyard Street

The Hildyard family link up with the Thorolds and with the village

74. Holme Street level crossing.

of Goxhill. In 1571 Elizabeth, daughter of Henry and Alice Welly of Gauxhill (sixteenth century spelling), married Sir Christopher Hildyard, Knight, of Yorkshire, by whom she had three sons.

Jump to the late eighteenth century and the Reverend William Thorold, Rector of Cuxwold and Ravendale (who died 1814) married Frances, daughter of William Hildyard of Goxhill. William Hildyard was George Babb's predecessor as Town Clerk. The Hildyards also owned land at Kelstern and Little Coates.

Holles Street

Named after Gervase Holles, an Alderman, whose family exerted considerable influence in the town from the 1600s. Gervase was Mayor

75. Hope Street, from Oxford Street, circa 1960.

76. Hope Street bluestone.

of Grimsby in 1636, 1638 and 1663. He is listed as an 'armiger', which means one who was privileged to bear arms; in other words, a gentleman.

He was also elected as an MP for the town in 1639 alongside Sir John Jacob.

Gervase was the grandson of another by the same name who had died in 1627 and had been the son of Frescheville Holles. He was interested in local antiquities and wrote many papers.

Alderman Gervase is alleged to have built the fort on the Barton Street for the defence of the area during the English Civil War.

Holme Street

Listed in the 1851 census. In 1852 there were twenty houses in the street and it was the site of the local gas works. There are several references in *Grimsby Free Press* and the *General Advertiser* between July and November 1860 to alterations to the railway crossing and the hindrance to traffic caused by delays in the work.

Bennett's Hall, built by William Bennett, father of Henry Bennett, was situated between Holme Street and East Marsh Street in East Gate, which no longer exists. The street's name originates from the fact that it led to the East Holme (*see* Welholme Road) and Holme Hall.

According to Shaw (1897) holme is an ancient word for a green place surrounded by water.

Hope Street (Lost)

This was originally called Charles Street, a name it kept until 1890. The change of name was said to have been made following one or two distressing incidents, which gave the street an unsavoury reputation. On 19 February 1889, a Maria Cave of 214 Charles Street died after losing consciousness. She had been involved in a struggle with an Elizabeth Harradine, housewife, during a quarrel about their children squabbling.

On 13 December 1889, a Mary Shannon was accidentally burnt to death. The report said she had been 'late residing in Hope Street'. The *Grimsby Observer and Humber News* on 28 March 1888 reported Mr Wintringham at a Cleethorpes Local Board meeting saying that 'it had been stated that the terraces in Charles St had been the means of spreading the disease of small pox'. A man kissed his girlfriend who had it, in spite of a warning from Mr Moody, Sanitary Inspector, and then returned to Charles Street, whence it was presumably carried to Cleethorpes Parish.

It was demolished in the late 1960s.

Humber Street

Named after its proximity to the River Humber.

Hume Street

This street begins by running off at a right angle southward from near the east end of Macauley Street, then it makes a right-angled turn to run parallel with Macauley Street, after which it turns at right angles again to West Parade. A final turn brings the explorer out into Littlefield Lane.

Hume Street and Macauley Street were named after two leaders of Liberalism in the mid–nineteenth century, Joseph Hume (1777-1855), Radical MP and advocate of Catholic Emancipation, and Thomas Babington Macauley – Lord Macauley – (1806-1859), the historian, poet, MP for Calne and Whig propagandist.

The streets were built circa 1872–5 and at that time Grimsby had

77. Intax House outbuildings, formerly a farm stood here.

two successive Liberal MPs in Henri Josse (1892) and Edward Heneage (1893). Hume Street, with its four right-angled turns, must be, topographically, the strangest in Grimsby.

Hunsley Crescent

At the time of the development of the Weelsby Park Estate, the St Andrew's Steam Fishing Company Limited owned an estate between Riplingham and High Hunsley in the East Riding of Yorkshire. One of the farms was known as Low Hunsley Farm, hence the name Hunsley Crescent.

Hutton Road

William Hutton represented Grimsby at a meeting of Manchester Sheffield & Lincolnshire directors on 14 February 1850. In 1860 he was one of a group of people to discuss business with the South Yorkshire Railway Company and was one of the first Manchester Sheffield & Lincolnshire directors to join the new Board in March 1861, after the South Yorkshire Railway had joined up with the M S & L.

By 1863 he was Lord Lieutenant of Grimsby and resigned from the board due to ill health in 1868 to be succeeded by his son, Lieutenant Colonel George Morland Hutton.

George M. Hutton was, in 1875, a member of the M S & L Locomotive Committee and in 1890 was one of five company directors in a committee to promote support for the company from industrialists and traders. He died on 11 February 1901.

Intax Farm Mews

Behind Welholme Galleries, this area is named after the farm that once stood here.

Jackson Street

William Jackson entered the Town Council in 1873. He was Mayor of Grimsby in 1881 and 1882. He seems to have retired from the council in 1907, but was still a borough magistrate in 1910.

In 1886, Miss Mary Jackson was Headmistress of South Parade Girls School, and J. L. Jackson was the House Surgeon for the Grimsby and District Hospital.

This street runs at the back of the Duke of York Gardens.

Joseph Street

This street was named after some prominent people in the town. Joseph Hewson entered the council (South West Ward) in 1896. In May 1905 he was made Alderman, and was Mayor 1905–6. He retired from the Council in 1899, but re-entered it in 1904.

Joseph Waltham Shepherd was elected to the council around 1895. By 1910 he had served on it for sixteen years and a Joseph Ward was Chairman of the Pastures Committee from 1904–05.

Keir Hardie Walk

Named after the Scottish socialist and Labour leader, Keir Hardie. Born

78. Kent Street.

in 1856 he is credited as being one of the founders of the independent Labour party, which in turn became the Labour party of today.

Kelham Road

Named after Kelham Hall near Newark in Nottinghamshire.

Kelstern Court

Named after a Lincolnshire airbase. The first airbase was here in the First World War when it was used as an emergency landing ground. In the Second World War it was home to 625 and 170 Squadrons.

Kensington Place

This Scartho street was built by T. W. Bygott, who had considered moving to St Helier in Jersey. Both Kensington Place and Rosaire Place were named after two residential streets in Jersey.

Kent Street

This street was one of the first streets to be built on the East Marsh and occupied by new settlers in the town after the development of the docks. Grimsby Corporation and the town's Freemen set out new roads on the East Marsh and leased them at a cheap rate.

These 'settlers' were fisherman enticed to come to the area after the building of the docks in the 1850s. Although many of them were from Hull, they originated from Kent and so chose to name the street after the county. *See* Freeman Street.

Though according to Cameron (1997), it was possibly named after an old Grimsby family called Kent from the 1540s.

Kesgrave Street

The following four names can be found on a map of Suffolk. Kesgrave, Levington and Nacton are villages near Ipswich where the Tomline family (see Tomline Street) had estates. Levington and Nacton are situated on the left bank of the River Orwell. *See also* Levington Street, Nacton Street, Riby Square and Orwell Street.

Kettlewell Street

This street is on the Heneage Estate. There was a shipping company called Kettlewell from Goole, that had connections with Grimsby in the early 1900s.

King Edward Street

The street is named in the 1893 book by Bates, which means it is not named after King Edward VII, who came to the throne in 1901 on the death of his mother, Queen Victoria. It could be Edward III, as under his reign the town thrived.

79. Lambert Road, modern view.

The street was in existence in the early 1800s, as it was part of a plot of land set out by the Corporation to help with the development and growth of the new dock. In the early years, the road had drains either side and was virtually impassable in winter. According to Bates the houses 'were poor and scattered, the vacant spaces being occupied as gardens'.

Split into North and South, the street contained seventeen 'buildings' with names like Toronto Place, Good's Buildings, Whitehall Yard, etc.

Knight Street

Named after the wife of the builder, Alec Cartledge, whose maiden name was Knight.

Laburnum Drive *see* Cherry Tree Crescent

Laceby Road

This name is self-explanatory, as it is the main road leading to the village of Laceby. At one time it did run through the village, until the traffic became too much and the A46 by-pass was built. Listed in 1457 as Lacebygate (Cameron).

Ladysmith Road

Since its extension to Weelsby Road after the Second World War, it has been one of the town's busiest thoroughfares. It is a Boer War souvenir,

General Redver Buller's relief of Ladysmith was one of the defensive events of the war (*see* Buller Street).

Lambert Road

In 1900 there was a scheme to make a road between two planned terraces in Welholme Road through the centre into Lambert Road. The terraces in the event were not built. Lambert Road marks the southern boundary of Wellow Abbey. However, it has been a struggle to find out who Lambert was; he could possibly have been the developer.

Lancaster Avenue

Was named after the late Alderman John William Lancaster, Mayor of Grimsby 1946–7. A printer by trade, he was elected councillor for the Humber Ward in 1926 and an Alderman in 1945. He retired from the Town Council in 1956.

This main civic interest was in public welfare. In 1919 he was appointed to the Board of Guardians for the Clee Ward. As a member of the Town Council he was for many years Chairman of the Welfare Services Committee. He was responsible for the opening of 3 Welholme Road as an additional Old People's Home in December 1952. He once said 'My wish is to see the Fryston and Claremont Homes opened. Then I shall be satisfied.' He died in 1967, aged 89.

Lansdowne Avenue

A ducal road named after the Marquess of Lansdowne. The roads in this part of town signify upmarket. *See also* Connaught Avenue.

Larmour Road

This road on the Willows Estate is named after Mr and Mrs M Larmour, who came to Grimsby in 1920 and left the town in 1975. Both were prominent members of the Labour Party, councillors, aldermen and Mayors of Grimsby.

Matthew Larmour was born in Lisburn. He was a foreman pattern-maker, was secretary

80. George Lister, chairman of the Grimsby Pasture Committee.

of Grimsby Labour Party for eleven years and was made Mayor in 1958. He left the council in 1974.

His wife, Margaret Larmour, came from Middlesborough. She entered the council four years before her husband and left it in 1970. She became Grimsby's first woman mayor in 1949, was the first woman to preside over the Director Sessions and the first person to have been both Mayor and Mayoress. The Larmours' special interest was in housing matters.

Legsby Avenue

Is one of the Heneage Estate streets. William White in his *History and Gazateer of Lincolnshire* (1856 edition) wrote, 'Legsby, or Legesby, a small ancient village on a bold acclivity of a picturesque dale, three miles south east of Market Rasen. George F. Heneage Esq., Sir R S Ainslie and some others have estates here.'

Levington Street

Village near to Orwell Park, Suffolk, home to Colonel Tomline, who owned the land in this area (*see also* Riby Square).

Lichfield Road

Named after the builder's residence. Mr S. Cartledge's father lived at 'Lichfield', a house in Bargate.

Lincoln Boulevard

This lies between Wells Street and the subway leading under the railway to Haycroft Avenue. It was named after the inimitable Bob Lincoln, builder, sportsman, leg-puller and writer of books about Grimsby. He lived at Cromwell House, 74 Cromwell Road.

For years, the south side remained half-finished and there was a 'green', crossed by tracks to Cromwell Road.

Lindsey Rise

This street was built by Mr T. W. Bygott. It was his intention to name it Stephen Rise after his son Stephen, but it was pointed out that there was a Stephen Crescent in Grimsby. So he re-named it Lindsey Rise, as the district was then in the Lindsey area of North Lincolnshire.

Linwood Avenue

Was first named Jutland Avenue before changing its name in the 1970s. Along with Beatty Avenue, it commemorated the Battle of Jutland fought in 1916. After the battle a number of wounded British sailors were brought to the Grimsby General Hospital for treatment. They included the boy hero, Jack Cornwell, V.C. After the war, Admiral Sir David Beatty was given the freedom of the borough. Linwood is a village near Market Rasen.

Lister Street

George Lister was Chairman of the Pastures Committee from 1900 to 1903, and also from 1906 to 1907. He died in 1909.

G. F. Lister was elected to the Pastures Committee in June 1904. W. G. Lister was the Headmaster of the Corporation Grammar School, having been appointed in 1899.

Littlefield Lane

Named after an area of the town referred to as Little Field, which is self-explanatory. The area was common pasture and owned by the Freemen.

Little John Street and Little Michael Street

Edmund Marshall built these two streets off Marshall Avenue and wanted to name them after his sons John and Michael. But there was already a John Street, so he had to name one Little John Street. Some official is said to have accidentally added the adjective 'little' to the intended name of Michael Street. The adoption dates are: Little John Street, 18 July 1934 and Little Michael Street, 1 October 1934.

Lombard Street

Situated off Spring Bank, it was named by Edmund Heelas, as was its neighbour Wall Street. He said he was thinking over financial speculations at the time. Adoption dates for both are 26 October 1939.

Lord Street *see* Ripon Street

Lower Spring Street

This street was split into Upper and Lower. In this area of town, off

Victoria Street, there was a spring, hence the name. The spring water, in later years, was used by Hewitt's Brewery.

Ludford Street

Named after the Lincolnshire village found near Hainton Hall owned by the Heneage family.

Ludlow Avenue

Named after the Shropshire market town close to the Welsh border. It has a beautiful castle.

Macauley Street *see* Hume Street

Maclure Street

Sir John William Maclure (1835–1901) was elected member of the Manchester Sheffield & Lincolnshire Board in 1864 and was a member of the M S & L Locomotive Committee in 1875. He was also a director of other railway companies. He was MP for Stretford (East Lancs) 1886–1901 and was known in the House of Commons as 'the white torpedo'; 'white' on account of the White Tor Line and 'torpedo' because his temperament was explosive.

W. G. P. Maclure was Locomotive Superintendant of the M S & L and in March 1896 of the Great Central Railway. He was very popular with the railwaymen and was said to know every driver and fireman by name.

Manor Avenue

It has posts at its west end, barring traffic into Manor Terrace and Brighowgate. Its name indicates the presence of a manor in feudal times. There was an old manor house in existence in 1892 near to Grosvenor Street and occupied by a Dr Stephenson, which probably stood on the site of an earlier one. Manor Avenue's adoption is dated as 7 Oct 1902.

Mansel Street

Believed to be named after John Maunsell Richardson, legendary racehorse trainer in the late 1800s and later, second husband to the dowager Countess of Yarborough on the death of her husband, the 3rd Earl of Yarborough, who was also his good friend.

Richardson was always called by his middle name, Maunsell, which was pronounced Mansel, as the street name is spelt. The couple lived at Healing Manor for some time before moving to Oakham, Rutland in 1902.

As a jockey, Maunsell won two Grand Nationals in the 1870s riding Disturbance and Reugny. He also was MP for Brigg in 1894.

Maple Avenue *see* Cherry Tree Crescent

Margaret Street

Off Hainton Avenue and named after the Hon. Margaret Heneage, daughter of Grimsby's MP in the 1880s, Edward Heneage.

Marsden Road

Derives its name from Sir John Marsden, Bart, JP. Introduced into the Grimsby business world as an accountant with Hagerup and Doughty by Sir George Doughty, in 1901. He was by 1924, Vice-chairman and Managing Director of the Consolidated Steam Fishing and Ice Company (Grimsby) Ltd, the largest trawler company in the world at that time, and also a director of the Grimsby Cordage Company (1924). In 1925 he was elected President of the British Trawlers Federation and held the position for about ten years. In January 1940 he was re-elected president and held the position until his death.

In 1942 he was appointed High Sheriff of Lincolnshire. He was also Squire of Panton, living at Panton Hall, where he died on 25 April 1944, aged 70. Before the First World War, he was an active playing member of the Grimsby Rovers Cricket Club.

Marshall Avenue

The late Edmund Marshall was a well-known builder in Grimsby between the First and Second World Wars. He named the avenue after his father, Christopher Marshall. The date of its adoption was 31 October 1933.

Marklew Avenue

This avenue honours Councillor Ernest Marklew. Born in Staffordshire, he worked first on a farm and then in the steel-rolling mill in Rotherham. He came to Grimsby about 1909 and became a fish merchant.

In 1914 he was elected leader of the Socialist Party of Grimsby and a town councillor in 1923. Six years later he unsuccessfully contested Grimsby in the parliamentary election. In 1935 he was elected MP for Colne Valley. He died on 14 June 1939 and his funeral service was conducted by his great friend, Canon Headley R. Burrows, one time Vicar of Grimsby. Marklew was a man of very sincere beliefs and was regarded as a most eloquent and effective public speaker. The street was adopted on 7 February 1935.

Maude Street

On 19 December 1831, Charles Anderson Worsley, 2nd Earl of Yarborough married the Hon. Maria Adelaide Maude, daughter of Cornwallis, 2nd Viscount Hawarden.

81. Moody Lane.

The 2nd Earl Yarborough died in 1862 and his wife remarried in 1869 to William Monson, 1st Viscount Oxenbridge. She died in 1897. Her son, Charles Anderson, became the 3rd Earl of Yarborough. The street was under construction in 1882 and commemorates her surname.

Meadow Court

Previous to the development being built, this area was a meadow bordering the River Freshney.

Medway Place

This road is named after the Kent area, which is home to Rochester Cathedral.

Mill Avenue

With its close proximity to where Dixons Paper Mill stood, it is likely

82. Centre Vale, Nelson Street.

that it is named after it. The mill was built by Peter Dixon and Son of Oughtibridge, Sheffield. It opened in 1909 and closed in 1973. It was once one of the largest in Europe and employed many people in the town.

Millom Way *see* Buttermere Way

Mirfield Road

Its name has an interesting origin. Houses on Mirfield Road were built by the late Mr Darnell. His son Harry, well known as an elocutionist on local concert platforms in the 1920s, had ambitions to enter the Church. His father gave him the choice of naming the street and he chose Mirfield, as he wished to attend the College of Resurrection at Mirfield, Yorkshire. Soon after this, he met the lady of his choice, married her, and abandoned his intention of becoming a priest.

Moody Lane

Existed until the 1970 alterations in the vicinity of St James's Church.

83. New Street.

It was situated between the east end of Chantry Lane and the south side of the Old Market Place, with shops on its south side in more modern times.

The Moody family was prominent in Grimsby in the early and mid nineteenth century. John Moody was Mayor in 1830 and Charles Bartholomew Moody was Mayor in 1850 and 1856. This quaint old street was also known as Rack's Passage.

In recent times, the name Moody Lane was given to a road on the Pyewipe Industrial Estate.

84. Central Market.

Nacton Street

Appears on the 1851 Census. It was named after a village near Orwell Park, home to Colonel Tomline, who also lived at Riby Hall (see Riby Square).

Naseby Drive *see* Winceby Avenue

Nelson Street

Named in honour of Admiral Horatio Nelson, whose greatest battle was the Battle of Trafalgar. *Also see* Wellington Street.

New Street

Appears on James Hollinsworth's plan of Grimsby in 1801. It was built on the original banks of the Haven, which flowed along New Street and Doughty Road, past the Old Cemetery to Wellow Mill.

It possessed one of the oldest buildings in the town, a Wesleyan Chapel built in 1837. In the 1970s, the chapel had been converted into

85. Nuns' Corner, circa 1900.

offices used by a local architect and Kirman's Chartered Accountants. One of the windows could be seen on the west, or Victoria Street side. In the hall of the offices was a hatchway or trapdoor, which, in olden days, covered a gully where the Haven waters used to run. It no longer stands.

New Cartergate

An extension of Cartergate, it was given the word New to differentiate it as it branched off the existing road. Can be found on the 1897 electoral register. *See* Cartergate.

Newhaven Terrace

Named after the Haven, into which the nearby River Freshney flows. New was added to differentiate it from Haven Street.

New Market Place (Lost)

Was the town's newest market place in the new town built around the 1850s on the East Marsh. Chapman's Hotel, run by Nathan Chapman, stood here. Renamed Central Market, before being demolished in the 1960s.

Newmarket Street

On the east side of the railway, its name is actually two words, New

86. Nuns' Farm.

Market, as it led to the new market place, later called Central Market, via the footbridge.

In 1899 next to the bridge was The Hippodrome, also known as The

87. Old Town Hall in the old Market Place.

88. Old Market Place 1860s.

89. Old Market Place, 1902.

Grand Circus. In 1907 it became a cinema. It was destroyed by fire on 24 August 1922.

The first footbridge was designed by a Mr Sacre, an engineer for the Manchester, Sheffield & Lincolnshire Railway in 1870 and was 600ft long and 6ft 3ins wide. It was estimated it would cost £2,000 (relative value in 2016 of £216,000) to build. It was replaced by the bridge we see today in 1955.

Newsham Drive

Built on land owned by the Yarborough family. Newsham Lodge and Bridge are part of the Brocklesby Estate.

Norwich Avenue

Another cathedral road. Norwich, in Norfolk, is home to a 900-year-old cathedral built in the Romanesque style.

Nuns' Corner

Named after St Leonard's Nunnery, which stood at this junction of two main roads, now occupied by the Grimsby Institute. The nunnery was established at the time of Henry I and was home to an order of Benedictine Nuns.

It was dissolved in 1543 and the lands became the property of the Earl of Yarborough. Following the nunnery, it became known as The Nuns' Farm House and was farmed until the 1950s, although the house was demolished sometime in the 1930s.

90. Osborne Street, 1865 a sketch of Beels' and Betts' pump by local artist George Skelton.

In 1962, the Grimsby Local History Society excavated the site. Some graves were found and were left in place with a dated lead tablet. Opposite the present site is the cenotaph, this stands on the spot known as Gallows Hill. It is believed this location is the site of the gallows, as it was the entrance to the town.

Old Market Place

The site of Grimsby's old market. Lost in development in the 1960s, though the name still remains.

Oliver Street (Lost)

This street no longer stands. It connected Ayscough Street and York Street with Fildes Street. It was named after the Reverend Dr George Oliver. In 1808 he was Master of the Grimsby Corporation Grammar School, became curate at St James's Church, Grimsby in 1814, and Vicar of Clee in 1815.

He wrote *The Byrde of Gryme* and *Monumental Antiquities of Grimsby,* but as Edward Gillett states, as an historian he was inaccurate and wildly imaginative. Politically he was a 'red' (Tory) and supported Charles Tennyson in the bitterly fought 1818 Parliamentary Election.

There is an Oliver Street in Cleethorpes.

Orwell Street

Named after Orwell Park, Suffolk, home to Colonel Tomline who owned land in this area (*see* Tomline Street and Riby Square).

Osborne Street

91. Pasture Street looking towards Victoria Street. The original Duke of Wellington pub is on the corner of Queen Street.

On early town maps, this street is called High Street. It is not shown in the 1855 directory, but is mentioned in the 1860 directory. Believed to have been named after a veterinary surgeon, Mr Osborne, though this is unsubstantiated.

Oxford Street

Possibly a ducal street, alongside some of the others in this area. Cleethorpes also has an Oxford Street and in his book *Street Names of Cleethorpes*, Dr Alan

92. Peaks field Avenue. A commemorative tower is inscribed '1911 Coronation Cottage' for the coronation of King George V.

Dowling says the Oxford Street in Cleethorpes was probably given a superior name to match the nearby Cambridge Street.

Pagehall Close

This Scartho street was named after the birthplace of the man who built the houses here. Mr C. Drew named it after his birthplace, Pagehall, a suburb of Sheffield.

Park Avenue

Named after People's Park, a 27-acre site given to the town by Edward Heneage, who was Grimsby MP from 1880–92 and 1893–95. Nearby is Park Drive.

Park Drive *see* Park Avenue

Park Street

Obviously derives its name from its proximity to Grant Thorold Park. It was constructed in the late 1880s. The *Grimsby News* of 7 November 1890 reports a Grimsby Highways Committee meeting at which it was stated that the road 'was in a shocking condition'.

A Councillor Nutt commented that people who chose to live in an 'undedicated' (unadopted) road could not expect the amenities offered to dedicated roads. The middle of the street, as far as its junction with

93. Peppercorn Walk.

94. Peppercorn crossing.

Wellington Street, and the north of it as far as Hamilton Street, marks the boundary between Grimsby and Cleethorpes.

Pasture Street

Again this street was named as it led to the town's pastures on the East Marsh.

Patrick Street

The name recalls another connection of the Heneages of Hainton with the Irish aristocracy (*see* Convamore Road), a very early one. An old copy of part of the Heneage genealogical table in the possession of the Grimsby Central Library shows that Jane Heneage, born in 1590, married the Right Honourable Patrick Plunkett, Baron Dunsany.

Peaks Field Avenue

Runs alongside the present day Peaks Parkway, though before that it was the main railway line. Named after the area, as up the road was

95. Pollitt Street, 1960. The houses on the left lead to the back-ways of Rowlandson Street, which is now the road to the fish docks.

Peaks Farm. *See* Highfield Avenue. The houses here were built in the early 1900s and there is a tower to commemorate this dated 1911.

Pelham Street

Takes its name from the family name of the Earls of Yarborough. The street was under construction in 1882. Pelham Terrace and Pelham

96. Pyewipe Cottages , at the end of Pyewipe Road on the Humber Bank

Road have the same name derivations. Pelham Terrace 'had just been erected in the early 1860s' (Lincoln Vol II) by the Earl of Yarborough. In Scartho there is also Pelham Avenue and Pelham Place, named for the same reason.

Pembroke Avenue

Pembroke Avenue, is named after the Welsh town.

Peppercorn Walk

Shaw (1897) provides the origins of this name. A cock fighting wager was set between Stephen de la See, Member for the borough and Sir John Empringham in 1445. The winner would give half an acre of land to the town for the purpose of an open cock-pit. In the end, Empringham's bird won and he gave the land, along with a pear tree, to the town, 'subject to the annual payment of a pound of unground pepper.' This gave the name to the place, Peppercorn.

The town's folk used the Peppercorn for recreational sports throughout the Middle Ages, archery being a common one.

Later, in 1855, Mr Chapman, chairman of Grimsby Borough Estates Committee, proposed that the town hall be built on 'the six acres field' owned by the Heneage family, if Heneage could be induced to open out the piece of land in front of it and make a street from the River Head to the six acres.

Heneage agreed, but Tennyson refused to give a road through his land, known as Peppercorn. If granted, it would have created a direct road from the six acres to Pasture Street through East Street.

There was a railway crossing on Peppercorn in 1891. Many accidents occurred at this crossing, so when the subway was opened in 1895 it was greeted with delight (*see* Doughty Road).

Pollitt Street (Lost)

Sir William Pollitt was Chief Clerk to the Manchester Sheffield & Lincolnshire Railway Company in 1869 and became the company's accountant in the 1870s. By 1894 he had become its general manager and in that year he produced a scheme to expand the No 2 Fish Dock at Grimsby.

Harry Pollitt was the M S & L Locomotive Engineer in the 1890s.

97. Ranter's Wharf, no longer standing. Victoria Flour Mill can be seen in the distance.

Pollitt Street was demolished in November 1971 (*see* Rowlandson Street).

Portland Avenue *see* Connaught Avenue and Eastwood Avenue

Prince's Avenue

Runs along the railway line and is reference to the Prince of Wales, later to become King Edward VII.

Pyewipe Road

Existed with the arrival of the railways and ran out to the Haven and Pyewipe Cottages – at one time possibly a public house and, later on, a rifle range.

Pyewipe is a corruption of the word, peewit, a bird of which there were plenty in the area. On some old maps it is called Pewit or Pewet.

Shaw (1897) recalls there being a Pyewipe Inn on the bank leading to Stallingborough Marshes.

Queen's Parade

Has a namesake in Cleethorpes. This runs along the railway line and is parallel to Prince's Avenue. Named in honour of Queen Victoria. Was originally known as Queen Street.

Quinton Road

Built circa 1930, it takes its name from Quinton, a suburb of Birmingham. The owner of the land where it was built was the Reverend Frank Bloomer, born at Quinton, where his family had business interests. He was appointed vicar of the St Augustine's Church, Grimsby in 1912. He died in 1938.

98. Red Hill, looking towards Flottergate, circa 1920.

Railway Street

This was always a rather grim street and few tears would be shed when the houses there were knocked down. In 1886 there was an 'eight foot road' there, with premises belonging to James Allen Christian, mineral water manufacturer, and John Edward Hazelgrove, printer.

99. Red Hill corner.

101. Riby House, Riby Square.

Ranter's Wharf (Lost)

This short street, running from the west side of Victoria Street to the Alexandra Dock, was so named from the fact that in the early and mid-

100. Riby Square, circa 1920.

nineteenth century, Grimsby non-conformists, who had the soubriquet 'Ranters' held open air camp meetings there.

Local folk artist John Connolly sings a song called Ranter's Wharf, based on this alley. It was lost in 1986 when it disappeared under what was MFI.

Ravenspurn Street

The remains of this street can be found between Corporation Road and Adam Smith Street. It is a reference to the lost village of Ravenser, sometimes written as Ravensrodd or Ravenspur, which was situated on Spurn Point, and was an important landing station pre-medieval times. It was eventually washed away by the sea in the fourteenth century.

Recto Avenue, Remillo Avenue, Reporto Avenue, Responso Avenue, Revigo Avenue and Rialto Avenue

These were named after the late Sir George Sleight's trawlers. Their names caused some critical comment when they were being built for being a sorting office nightmare! Sleight had bought the land from the Heneage estate in the early 1900s.

Red Hill (Lost)

Named after a political party – the Reds, which was a nickname for the Tories in the eighteenth century. It ran along the back of the present top town market (Flottergate) towards Cartergate. Its real name was Pinfold Hill.

Rendel Street

Commemorated James Meadows Rendel (1799-1856) the civil engineer who, assisted by Adam Smith, planned and built the Royal Dock. He also made a map of Grimsby in 1848.

The *Grimsby Gazette* in November 1853 mentioned a steam tug, *Rendel* operating in the docks.

Revesby Avenue

Named after Revesby Abbey, a Cisterician religious house in the Lincolnshire village of the same name. Founded in 1143 by William D'Aubigny, First Earl of Lincoln, it was dissolved by Henry VIII and became a house lived in by naturalist Joseph Banks. Nearby is Crowland Avenue.

Riby Square

Riby Hall, on the outskirts of town, was for many years the seat of the Tomline family. In 1848 George Tomline built a school and four almshouses at Riby. The last of the Tomline family bequesthed his estate and name to the late Dr Pretyman, Bishop of Lincoln 1787–1820, who assumed the name of Tomline.

In 1868 George Tomline was returned as MP for Grimsby.

Riby Street *see* Riby Square

Richard Street

Another of the councillor streets. Councillor Richard Guy Kitching was a member of the Pastures Committee 1913. Councillor Richard Johnson was elected for the South West Ward in 1899. He served for at least twelve years. In the decade 1910–20 he lived in West Parade.

102. Robinson Street, showing number 8 where Sir George Doughty MP was born, on left hand of passage.

Ripon Street

Named after the Lord Lieutenant of Lincolnshire in the 1860s, Earl de Grey and Ripon. Grimsby's new Town Hall was officially opened by a banquet given by the Mayor, Henry Bennett, on 15 October 1863 but Earl de Grey and Ripon was unable to attend according to Lincoln Vol I (p 414).

Roberts Street

A number of streets in this area have connections with the Boer War, Ladysmith Road, Durban Road and Buller Street. Roberts Street is named after Field Marshal, Earl Roberts who had seen military success in the Indian War. In the South African wars he was in command of the British troops before being succeeded by Lord Kitchener.

Robinson Lane

Sited on the docks Robinson Lane commemorates Sir Thomas Robinson, KBE (1855–1927) a most prominent figure in the Grimsby fishing industry. He went to sea aged 14 as a cabin boy on the old fishing smacks and went on to become the owner of a fleet of trawlers. In the First World War he was adviser to the Board of Fisheries and a member of the Food Control Committee. Later he became Consultancy Director of the Canadian Fish and Cold Storage Co. He was also Hon Treasurer of the Primitive Methodist Orphanage for twenty years, a JP, a member of Lincolnshire County Council and Chairman of the Lindsey Education Committee.

He was a director of the Coal, Salt and Tanning Co. from 1904 to 1913 and chairman of the Onward and Dominican Steam Fishing Co, the Steam Trawler Coals and Trading Co, and the Lincolnshire Insurance Co.

Robinson Street

Had four inhabitants (or householders) in 1860. It appears on a map of 1863 and in the PO Directory of Grimsby and Cleethorpes in 1886.

Found as East Robinson Street and believed to have been named after a Grimsby family, Robynson, found in various Grimsby records from the 1500s.

Ropery Street

Bob Lincoln (Vol 1 p179) wrote 'in 1889 machine-made twine had become such a strong competitor to the hand-made article that it was destined to form the Cordage Company, and the factory was erected in this year.'

In 1901 the Grimsby Cordage Company was formed. Its directors were Charles Jeffs, Edwin Bacon, C. F. Carter, William Grant, George E. J. Moody, Harrison Mudd, William S. Letten and Henry Smethurst. The whole of the company's premises were built up on freehold land in Ropery Street.

Rosaire Place *see* Kensington Place

Roseveare Avenue

Was also built by J. H. Thompson and Sons Ltd. It was named after

Major Leslie Roseveare who was, for the years 1920-40, the Borough Engineer of Eastbourne, for whom the firm had completed a number of housing projects.

Rosina Grove

Was named after Mrs Steel, sister of a local builder Sam Cartledge and daughter of the late Mr Sam Cartledge.

Roundway

Was another street built on land owned by the late Sir Alec Black. Its name means exactly what it says. It is a street which curves round almost in a circle. It was built in the late 1930s.

Rowlandson Street

C A Rowlandson was Resident Engineer for the Manchester Sheffield & Lincolnshire Railway Company in the 1809s for the 'London End'. In 1896 he was appointed engineer for the company.

The street was demolished in the 1970s when Pollitt Street went. Both were built circa 1850 to house skippers and crews of fishing boats based at Grimsby and owned by the railway company. The name still exists as the entrance to the docks.

Rutland Street

Was originally named Corden Street. The name was altered so it would match other ducal street names, such as Grafton Street and Hamilton Street in that part of town and possibly to avoid confusion with Cobden Street.

Corden was an unsuccessful candidate at the Grimsby Municipal

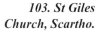

103. St Giles Church, Scartho.

Election of 1855. The road was called Corden Street in 1880 and adopted in 1892. An extension of Rutland Street was adopted in 1902.

Sackville Street

Named after the Hon. Sackville George Anderson-Pelham who became the fifth Earl of Yarborough in 1936 when his father, the fourth Earl died. When he subsequently died on February 7 1948, the title passed to his brother Marcus. Sackville's older brother, Charles had been killed in the First World War.

Sanctuary Lane

No longer in existence as it lies underneath the modern shopping precinct. In the vicinity of the Augustinian Friary dissolved by Henry VIII – hence the likelihood of its name. Listed in 1594 as Sanckuarye Layne. On the junction with Flottergate stood the very fine Georgian, Flottergate House, which was demolished in the 1960s as part of Grimsby's modernisation.

Seascale Walk *see* Buttermere Way

St Andrew's Drive

This has Hull fishing connections. The Weelsby Park Estate was developed by Ashridge Farms Limited, which became a subsidiary company of St Andrew's Steam Fishing Company Limited. In 1967 it changed its name to Boston Deep Sea Fisheries Limited. St Andrew's Dock is in Hull.

St Andrew's Drive obtained its name from the original holding company.

St Augustine Avenue

Is another street connected with Wellow Abbey, which had a dual dedication to St Augustine and St Olaf (*see* St Olaf's Grove).

Wellow Abbey was often referred to in old documents as Grimsby Abbey. Henry I founded it about 1110 as a house of Augustinian Canons.

St Giles Avenue

This gets its name from St Giles Church, Scartho, which has an Anglo-Saxon tower. St Giles was a very popular dedication of the eleventh century. The first person to buy a building plot here was Harry Emerson so he was given the opportunity to name the street and named it after the nearby church.

St James Avenue

Named after the Parish church. St James was made a Minster in 2010.

St Mary's Gate, East, West, South and North

These streets enclosed the Church of St Mary, which was demolished around 1585 and its parish united with St James's. The site comprised about two acres and was seen as the mariner's church.

Gervase Holles stated that the church was a fine, very large Gothic structure with a lofty tower, which mariners used as a beacon to guide them into the Old Haven.

In 1553 Francis Ayscough wrote to Sir William Cecil suggesting that the church be demolished as it was in such a state of disrepair. The church site remained undeveloped from 1585 to 1801. North St Mary's Gate was incorporated into Baxtergate.

In 1776 the old churchyard was leased to the Pelhams 'for three lives' by the Vicar of Grimsby, but at the Lammas Assizes at Lincoln in 1822, Dr Tennyson brought an action to prevent Yarborough using it, as it

104. Scartho Road workhouse.

would constitute an injury to the interests of the successors of 'Rest Rowling', Clergyman. The action was unsuccessful.

St Michael's Road

This road is off Little Coates Road to the west. Little Coates Parish Church is dedicated to St Michael.

St Olaf's Grove

This is a small street off Abbey Drive East. Wellow Abbey was dedicated to St Olaf and St Augustine. The ancient seal of the Abbey shows two figures said to be the two saints. St Olaf was also King Olaf II of Norway from AD 1016 to 1030. This dedication to a Norwegian hints at something that other sources also suggest: Grimsby may have had a Norwegian and not a Danish origin.

Stanage Walk

Based in the East Marsh. Named after the Derbyshire area of beauty.

105. Silver Street, July 1965. Jackson, Green and Preston's auction rooms are at the end of the street.

Samuel Avenue

Named after Samuel Cartledge, son of the builder of the same name.

Saunders Street

Samuel Saunders of East Marsh Street, a freeman of Grimsby and member of the Freeman's Committee in 1882, was a member of the Pastures Committee elected on June 1904 and served until 1909.

Scampton Close

Another road named after a Lincolnshire village and airbase. Scampton was home to 617 'Dam Busters' Squadron. Wing Commander Guy Gibson led the raids on the dams in the Ruhr Valley. The base is currently home to the RAF's display team, the Red Arrows.

106. Brocklesby Mausoleum where lies Sophia Aufrere, wife of Charles Anderson, 1st Baron of Yarborough. Sophia was a popular family name. Sophia Avenue is named after them.

Scartho Road

This is a self-explanatory road, as it is one of the main arterial roads into Grimsby starting in the village of Scartho, which is now seen as a suburb of the town.

Sheepfold Street

Near Pasture Street and named after where the sheepfold was sited. Listed in the 1851 Census according to Cameron.

Sherwood Road

Named after the Sherwood district of Nottinghamshire. Nearby roads are named after religious houses.

Silver Street

One of Grimsby's oldest streets and only part of it survives today. In 1775 a Calvinist Chapel was built on the left hand side near Sanctuary Lane (now no longer). Fourteen people were buried there, the first in 1785 and the last in 1826. This chapel then became a Temperance Hall and continued as such until 1852.

This was later replaced by the old Church of England School, built by Canon Ainslie, but many will remember it as Jackson and Green's auction room. Lincoln (1913) states 'opposite of St Mary's Church was a venella [narrow Lane] called Swan Lane which stretched northward over the Swan Bridge and formed a junction with Flete Street near the Haven … the dimensions of Swan Lane have been considerably reduced in modern times, but it is now an important street known as Silver Street.'

107. Stanley Street.

Sixhills Street

Another street deriving its name from the Heneage Estate. William White (1856) describes Sixhills as 'an ancient village on a bold eminence 4½ miles east by south of Market Rasen, belonging to G F Heneage Esq., the lord of the manor.'

Sophia Avenue

Sophia is a traditional name in the Earl of Yarborough's family over the centuries. In the village of Great Limber stands the Brocklesby Mausoleum, built by James Wyatt between 1787 and 1794 to commemorate the death of Sophia Aufrere, wife of Charles Anderson, 1st Baron Yarborough. She died aged 33. The mausoleum is based on the Temples of Vesta at Rome and Tivoli.

In 1886 the 4th Earl married Sophia, Baroness Fauconberg and Conyers. See Fauconberg Avenue and Conyers Avenue.

Sophia Avenue is in Scartho, where it runs off Pelham Avenue.

South Parade

This street was an extension of the public promenade constructed along the banks of the Freshney (*see* Freshney Street and Haven Avenue) and planted with trees in 1877. Grimbarians could walk along the

108. Strand Street in the 1940s.

109. Stortford Street, showing Ena Terrace. No date.

promenade, past the front of the new hospital (now the former General Hospital) and via South Parade (which faced south) into Alexandra Road – South Parade School was opened in 1895. The foundation stone of the South Parade Board School was laid in 1879.

Spark Street

Found off Spring Bank and is evidence of the builder's sense of humour. Edward Heelas constructed houses here and bestowed the name Spark Street, as there was a big electricity grid in the street. Its adoption date was 23 November 1959.

Spencer Street

This street is just inside Grimsby. It lies on the north side of Park Street, between Cleethorpe Road and Stirling Street. It has houses on the south side only, the north side being formed by the back gardens of Stirling Street.

Its name may have a connection with the Yarborough Estate streets.

It is near to Victor Street, which is a Yarborough Estate street. Edith Charlotte, daughter of Captain Dudley Worsley Pelham (second son of the 2nd Earl Yarborough), married Captain Gilbert Spencer Smith, late 85th Light Infantry on 10 August 1875 (*see also* Hilda Street /Stirling Street).

Springfield Road

A relatively new road in Scartho connecting to the Springfield Estate. Named after the fact there were mineral water springs in the field.

Stanley Street

Another street with political connections. Named after Frederick Arthur Stanley, 16th Earl of Derby and son of the Prime Minister Edward Stanley. Frederick Stanley was born in 1841 and died in 1908. Between 1886 and 1893 he was known as Lord Stanley of Preston and was a member of the Conservative Party. He was President of the Board of Trade and Secretary of State for War.

Stansted Street *see* Gilbey Road

Stephen Crescent

Built by Harry Smith, who named it after his son.

Stirling Street

Connected with the Grant-Thorold family. It was probably named after Admiral Sir James Stirling, whose daughter was grandmother of Lieutenant Colonel E. A. Spencer, who married Hilda Grant-Thorold. *See* Hilda Street.

Strand Street

The name reminds us that the area from Lock Hill to Cleethorpes was a shore over 100 years ago. It is mentioned in the *Grimsby Observer* of 3 April 1872. It also mentions in May 1872, 'property in Strand Street, formerly Bath Street.'

Stortford Street *see* Gilbey Road

Surtees Street

Named after Colonel Charles Freville Surtees, who was elected to the

110. Thesiger Street.

Manchester Sheffield & Lincolnshire Board of Directors on 28 March 1890. At that time he was also a director of the South Eastern Railway Company. He died on 22 December 1896.

Sutcliffe Avenue

Alderman Jack Sutcliffe was Mayor of Grimsby 1896 and 1897. He died in 1913. He was succeeded by Tom Sutcliffe in directing the firm's business. Tom was also MP for Grimsby 1922 and 1923 and a High Sheriff of Lincolnshire in 1929. He lived at Stallingborough Manor. Tom's sister, Kate, married Grimsby architect, Ernest Farebrother. *See* Farebrother Street.

Swinderby Gardens

Named after a Lincolnshire village and airbase. RAF Swinderby was home to 300 and 301 Polish bomber squadrons in the Second World War. The base was closed in 1993 and the land sold in 1995.

Sycamore Avenue

This avenue off Scartho Road has a link with Chestnut Avenue, off Wells

Street. On 2 September 1929, plans were presented to the Grimsby Town Council Highways Committee by Mr C W Dixon and agreed for 'three streets in the two fields in front of the Institution on the west side of Scartho Road. The streets are to be named Chestnut Avenue, Beech Avenue and Lime Tree Avenue.'

It was later pointed out that there was already a Chestnut Avenue in Grimsby and Sycamore was given instead.

Tasburgh Street

Lying off Hainton Avenue, and close to the junction with Welholme Road, it is named after the maiden name of Edward Heneage's mother, Frances. Edward was Grimsby's MP in 1880 and one of the major landowners in the town. Frances Tasburgh died in 1842.

Tattershall Avenue

Named after the Lincolnshire village where stands a fine castle built by Ralph Cromwell in 1434. The castle is built from red brick and is owned by the National Trust.

Thesiger Street

The clue to the name is to be found in the *Skelton Diaries* written by William Skelton and his wife.

In the *Skelton Diaries*, on 9 and 10 February 1848, there is recorded a trial at the Town Hall between the Freemen of Grimsby and the Manchester, Sheffield and Grimsby Railway Company to assess the amount of compensation to be made to the Corporation for land in the East Marsh, Little Field and Haycroft belonging to the Freemen. Sir Frederick Thesiger was retained on behalf of the Corporation and compensation awarded by the jury was £17,000.

The street is 970ft long and 45ft wide.

Thirkleby Crescent

Derives its name from the fact that when the Weelsby Park Estate was developed, an agricultural property at Kirby Grindalythe near Thirkleby in Yorkshire was owned by the St Andrew's Steam Fishing Company Limited.

111. New town Hall, Town Hall Street.

Thomas Street

Named after Reverend Thomas Heneage, son of Edward. Thomas succeeded his brother George to the Heneage title in 1954; he died in 1967.

Thorold Street

Named after Richard Thorold, of Weelsby. It was one of the streets laid out in Thorold's Enclosure Land. Richard Thorold was High Sheriff of the County of Lincoln in 1829. He was a Provisional Director of the Grimsby Pier Company in 1836 and Chairman of the Grimsby Dock Company in 1845.

Tomline Street

In 1868 George Tomline was elected MP for Grimsby, defeating John Fildes (*see also* Riby Square). A gale in August 1833 destroyed more than half of the properties that had been built between Riby Street and the Humber Hotel by George Harris in 1831. The mortgagees sold the land on which it was built and the buyer resold to Colonel Tomline for £20,000.

112. Questor Veal.

The Dock Company and Colonel Tomline fought a legal battle over its possession. Eventually the Dock Company bought the fourteen acres of land awarded to Tomline by the Commissioners of Woods and Forests for £20,000.

Tomline Street runs from Cleethorpes Road to Orwell Street.

Toothill Road

Named after the area it is in – Toothill – said by Oliver (1825) to be a corruption of a Celtic chieftain's name, Tuut. Oliver claims there was a barrow in the vicinity and there is a photograph dating from the nineteenth century showing people digging out a mound.

Torrington Street

Its name was adopted from the villages of East and West Torrington, near Wragby, on the original Hainton estate.

It also has connections with the Turnor and Ainslie families. In the

113. Veal Street.

1850s Christopher Turnor owned most of East Torrington and Sir Robert Ainslie was Lord of the Manor of West Torrington.

Town Hall Street

Runs in front of the Grimsby Town Hall, built in 1863, which replaced the old Town Hall sited near to St James Church, which had been built in 1780. It was built in the modern Italian style. The building signified the prosperity the town enjoyed at the time of its building.

Tranby Drive

The origin of the name is a farm on the outskirts of Hessle in East Yorkshire called Tranby Park Farm, originally owned by the Hewitt Estate of Grimsby and purchased by the Boston Deep Sea Fisheries Limited from the Hewitts in 1942 along

114. St Anthony's Orphanage, Victor Street.

115. Victoria Street west, 1900s.

116. Nautical College, Victoria Street near to Lock Hill.

117. 'Victoria Street looking east with the Savoy Cinema in the background.'

with the rest of the Hewitt Estate, near Grimsby, of which the Weelsby Park Estate formed a part.

Tunnard Street

Another of the Thorolds' Enclosure Land streets. This street was named after Frances Tunnard, the daughter and heiress of Samuel Tunnard of Boston, who owned land and lived in a mansion built in 1720. She married Richard Thorold of Weelsby (*see* Thorold Street). The street was adopted in 1892.

Utterby Drive

Named after the Lincolnshire village four miles from Louth.

Vaughan Avenue

At its eastern end it reaches the border with Cleethorpes. It commemorates Captain Vivian Vaughan Hewitt (*see* Vivian Avenue), a member of the Hewitt brewing dynasty. William Taylor Hewitt of Hewitt's Brewery lived at Weelsby Old Hall and died on 8 April 1902. His successor, Thomas William Good Hewitt, died at Weelsby Old Hall on 9 May 1930. He was a generous benefactor to the Grimsby Rural District. T. W. G. Hewitt was uncle to Captain Hewitt.

Veal Street

Commemorates a family prominent in the civic life of Grimsby for fifty years in the nineteenth century.

Questor Veal, as a 'Common Council Man' was one of the committee of nine appointed in April 1827 to enquire into the Rights of the Burgesses of Great Grimsby on the 'enclosure of the different commonable fields' and was Mayor of Grimsby in 1831.

He was also the first manager of the branch set up in the town by the Hull Banking Company in 1835. He conducted his banking business in his office behind No 4 Flottergate.

Henry James Veal was Mayor of Grimsby in 1877, 1878, 1887 and 1888.

118. Watkin Street.

Victor Street

This street was in existence in 1880 and was probably named after the 3rd Earl of Yarborough's second son, Captain Hon. Victor Pelham, born in 1866, for other streets in the town are named after the family. When built, it was intended to be an alternative major road to the docks from

119. Hainton Halt on Welholme Road.

Weelsby Road and the south-east. It is one of the original Yarborough Estate streets (*see also* Albert Street).

Victoria Street

Was originally known as Loft Street and part of it was known as Baxtergate until 1854, when it became Victoria Street on the occasion of the visit of Queen Victoria and the Prince Consort on 14 October 1854. At the same time, the railway company's recently constructed dock was re-christened the Royal Dock.

Its original name of Loft Street came from Major General John Henry Loft, when he became MP for the borough in 1807. He lost his seat in 1812. Major Loft lived at Louth and Healing during his time as MP. He died in Grimsby in 1849, aged 82 and is buried at Marshchapel.

Vivian Avenue *see* Vaughan Avenue

The land in this area was once owned by the Hewitt family, famous in the town for the brewery. Captain Vivian Vaughan Hewitt was the nephew of William Taylor Hewitt, a great benefactor to the town. Vivian Avenue runs between Vaughan Avenue and Weelsby Road.

Captain Hewitt was famous for being an aviation pioneer and was the first person to fly across the Irish Sea in 1912 – a distance of seventy-five miles. This was further than Louis Bleriot, who is credited as being the first to fly across the English Channel – a distance of only twenty-

120. Wellowgate Crossing.

five miles; unfortunately, Captain Hewitt's greatest flying triumph was overshadowed by the sinking of the Titanic.

Born in 1888, he moved to Bodfari, North Wales in 1902 on the death of his father. The Welsh village was the home of his mother's family. He died in 1965.

Waddington Place

Situated just off Coningsby Drive, this street is named after a Lincolnshire village and airbase. Waddington was home to the Vulcan bombers and is home to reconnaissance aircraft, the E3D Sentry.

Watkin Street

Built in 1882, it takes its name from Sir Edward William Watkin, MP and chairman of the Manchester Sheffield & Lincolnshire Railway Company for many years. He was active in the development of Grimsby as a port, particularly with concern to the Old and Royal Docks and the construction of the Alexandra Dock.

Alfred Mellor Watkin was MP for Grimsby in 1877. The street is split in half by Armstrong Street and known as Watkin Street North and South.

121. Westlands House.

Welbeck Place and Welbeck Road

Possibly named after Welbeck Spring on Barton Street near to the English Civil War fort and an Anglo-Saxon burial ground. Lincoln (1853) says, 'a steeplechase meeting was held on March 8th near the Laceby Cross Roads the winning post being at the foot of the hill in the Welbeck Spring field.' Welbeck is also a religious house near Newark and ties in with other roads in the vicinity.

Welholme Road

Is said to be so named because it was originally the old Wellow Abbey road running from the Abbey to the East Holmes (or small hills, e.g. Holme Hill), which was found in the East Marsh and district. There was no Welholme Road in 1883.

Welland Avenue

Named after the River Welland, which starts in Northamptonshire and flows to The Wash. It stretches sixty-five miles long. *See* Crowland Avenue.

Wellington Street

The street appears in the *Grimsby and Cleethorpes Directory* 1880.

In 1872, the Wellington Building Society had fifty houses built here at a cost of £110 each, and it is likely the street was named after them.

This road runs from Queen Mary Avenue to Freeman Street.

Wellowgate

This is another of the town's ancient roads, which ran from the former Wellow Abbey to St James's Church (*See* Abbey Road). Wellow means a spring by a hill or mound and in Oliver's book (1825) he talks of Abbey Hill measuring ten acres. Of course Wellow Abbey Gate stems from the Danish – gata – meaning street. The name Wellow also survives today as an area of the town, although at one time it was a hamlet and not part of Grimsby.

Wellow Abbey was founded in the time of King Henry I and was a house for the Augustinian Canons. It was dedicated to St Olaf and St Augustine and was finally dissolved by King Henry VIII in 1539. Residents here have uncovered bodies when carrying out work, so presumably it was part of the Abbey burial ground.

Wells Street

On its north side are ten houses built about 1908; on its south side there are two houses, which faced the former building works and offices of Messrs J. W. Thompson. In Bates (1893) it clearly shows there are blow wells on the west side of the Hay Crofts in approximately the same area where Wells Street stands today.

In 1855 the Freemen considered leasing an acre of land for ninety-nine years in the Hay Croft Pastures as a site for the Waterworks Company, 'the precise position at the corner of Cromwell Road and Wells Street'.

Westlands Avenue

Named after Westlands House, which stands at the end of this Avenue and at one time was home to Sir Henry Bennett, timber merchant and ship owner. He had the house built in 1875 for his new bride, Sophia.

Westminster Drive *see* Canterbury Drive

Westward Ho

Named after the Devon seaside resort. This road was formerly called Ely Road, which was in keeping with the other roads in the vicinity named after cathedrals. However, because Ely Road ran into Cambridge Road, the council renamed it in the late 1960s to avoid confusing people.

Wharncliffe Road

Commemorates the prominent director of the Manchester Sheffield & Lincolnshire Railway Company, which was eventually merged into the Great Central Railway Company.

James Archibald Stuart Wortley, 1st Baron Wharncliffe (1776–1845), was head of the Provisional Committee to form the Manchester Sheffield & Lincolnshire Railway Company in 1836.

He was a director of the Sheffield, Ashton-under-Lyne and Manchester Railway Company, which eventually merged into the Manchester Sheffield & Lincolnshire.

The 3rd Baron Wharncliffe was a member of the Manchester Sheffield & Lincolnshire board in 1864. In 1890 he became its deputy chairman and was finally appointed chairman in 1894, from which position he resigned in 1899 on account of ill health.

Wharton Street

Thomas William Wharton served as Chairman of the Pastures Committee in 1867 and also as a committee member in 1868 and 1869. J. Wharton was auditor of the Freemen's Committee in 1882.

Whitgift Street (Lost)

Named after one of Grimsby's famous sons – John Whitgift, who was made Archbishop of Canterbury in 1583 by Queen Elizabeth I. His uncle Robert was Abbott of Wellow and he looked after the future Archbishop's early education. It is said that Whitgift was there by her bedside when the queen died and that he crowned King James I. Though Whitgift Street no longer exists, there is a Whitgift Close in Laceby.

Wymark View

Named in honour of Patrick Wymark, the famous stage and television actor, who was born in Cleethorpes on 11 July 1926. His real name was Patrick Carl Cheeseman. He took his acting name from his grandfather-in-law.

Wymark was educated at Wintringham Grammar School and after

university went to the Old Vic Theatre School. His film roles include *Children of the Damned (1964)* and *Where Eagles Dare (1968)*.

In 1964 he was named Best TV Actor of the year by the Guild of Television Producers and Directors for his role as the tycoon in ATV's *The Plane Makers*. On 6 April 1965, he was given a civic reception by the Mayor of Grimsby.

He died in Melbourne, Australia in 1970 aged 44.

Wickenby Close

Named after a Lincolnshire village but also an airbase from the Second World War. It was a satellite airfield used by Lancaster squadrons 12 and 626.

Wickham Road

Named after J. A. Wickham, Chief Engineer for docks to the London and North Eastern Railway Company, when number three Fish Dock was built.

Wickham had been largely responsible for designing the new dock, which opened in 1934. He sadly died in April 1930 before work on the docks had even begun. As a result, the project was considerably delayed; work eventually began in November 1930.

The new dock, financed largely by the Old Corporation was opened in October 1934. Mr Wickham is mentioned with honour in the souvenir handbook and it is entirely fitting that his name should be perpetuated in a street beside the dock, which owed so much to him.

Willingham Street

Named after the Lincolnshire village near the Heneage Estate at Hainton.

122. Woodrow Park's former gates.

Willoughby Grove

This street is named after the Lincolnshire village near Alford. Its famous resident was Captain John Smith, who was one of the leaders of the Virginia Colony in America. He is linked with the Native American Indian, Pocahontas.

Winceby Street

Could be called a continuation of Cromwell Road, on the western side of Boulevard Avenue subway. It is well named, linking with Oliver Cromwell, who won the Battle of Winceby, fought near Horncastle, against the Cavaliers in 1643. The site of the battle is still known as Slash Lane. It is also a nature reserve. Naseby Drive, another English Civil War battle is nearby.

Wintringham Road

Named after a number of Mayors of Grimsby bearing the name Wintringham. John Wintringham (1864-65); Thomas Wintringham (1870-71); and John Wintringham (1874). The Wintringham family was very prominent in Grimsby politics. In 1901, a John Fildes Wintringham, a solicitor, lived in Danesbury House in Bargate.

Womersley Road

The Rt. Hon. Sir Walter Womersley, Bart., PC, JP and MP for Grimsby (1924–1945). His greatest achievement was his work in helping to provide the town with Number 3 Fish Dock in 1934.

He was a redoubtable champion of the fishing industry, especially Grimsby's and was nicknamed 'Fish' Womersley in the House of Commons.

In the Government, he served as Junior Lord of the Treasury and was Parliamentary Private Secretary to Sir Kingsley Wood, Secretary of the Board of Education. He also was Assistant Postmaster General (1935–1939).

As Minister for Pensions from 1939 he was the only government minister to hold the same office throughout the Second World War.

He was knighted in 1934 and received a baronetcy in 1945, when he lost his seat. In 1950 he was made High Sheriff of Grimsby and was the first secretary of the Grimsby Chamber of Trade. In 1922 he had been Mayor of Grimsby and was also a senior partner in a local firm of jewellers. He died in March 1961, aged 83.

Wood Street

Like Duncombe Street, it runs off Freeman Street and gets its name from former Grimsby MP, Charles Wood, who was elected with George F. Heneage on 17 June 1826. He was re-elected with George Harris on 31 July 1830.

Woodrow Park

Built in the 1970s and named after Woodrow Hall, which had once stood on the site. The hall was built in 1860 and was lived in by the Bacon family, who were trawler owners. On Scartho Road near to the roundabout, there is a section of walling and gate posts; set into the wall there is a stone bearing the name of the lost house.

Worcester Avenue

Part of the Cathedral streets. Named after Worcester Cathedral, which was founded as a monastery in AD 680; building of the cathedral itself was started by Bishop Wulfstan in 1084, it was eventually dissolved by Henry VIII. *See* Gloucester Avenue and Hereford Avenue.

Worsley Street (Lost)

This street disappeared in the 1970s, when the predecessor to Freshney Place was built. It connected Sanctuary Lane with Victoria Street and got its name from Lord Worsley, the title always given to the Earl of Yarborough's eldest son. It was one of Grimsby's oldest streets and in 1852 it had eighteen households.

Wragby Street

Named after the Lincolnshire village, near to Hainton, home of the Heneages. It lies just off Fraser Street.

Yarborough (Street) Drive/Yarborough Road

This street was built in 1882. It was not joined to neighbouring Earl Street by the bridge until 1884. The 'street' is no longer, having been renamed Yarborough Drive following the redevelopment of the area when the old General Hospital was demolished in 1985. It is not to be confused with Yarborough Road. The names of these two thoroughfares are after the Brocklesby family and the title, Earl of Yarborough. At one time the family had strong connections with the town. *See* Freshney Drive

Yarrow Road

This road was no doubt named after the plant, yarrow. Prior to development in the 1970s, this area was open meadow.

York Street

In 1877 a public promenade was planted along the banks of the River Freshney, near the old General Hospital. In later years the town would receive People's Park (1883) and in 1893 the Corporation created the Duke of York's Gardens in the West Marsh.

The Duke of York Gardens celebrated the wedding of the Duke to Princess Mary and were officially opened by the Mayor, George Doughty and his wife. The eight-acre site included a children's recreation ground and a cycle track.

York Street is in the immediate vicinity and is named after the Duke.

Illustrations and Acknowledgements

This book has seen me helped by a number of people including Jennie Mooney and the staff at Grimsby Central Library's Reference Library; John Wilson, former North East Lincolnshire archivist and the *Grimsby Telegraph*. Photograph(s) reproduced courtesy of North East Lincolnshire Library Service, Lincs Inspire Ltd (1, 2, 3, 6, 7, 8, 9, 11, 12, 13, 15, 16, 17, 18, 19, 20, 21, 22, 23, 24, 25, 26, 27, 28, 29, 30, 31, 32, 33, 34, 35, 37, 38, 39, 40, 41, 42, 43, 44, 45, 46, 48, 49, 50, 53, 54, 55, 56, 57, 58, 59, 60, 61, 62, 63, 64, 65, 67, 68, 70, 71 72, 73, 74, 75, 76, 77, 83, 84, 85, 86, 87, 88, 89, 90, 91, 93, 94, 95, 96, 97, 98, 99, 100, 101, 102, 104, 105, 107, 109, 110, 111, 113, 114, 115, 16, 117, 118, 119, 120, 121); *Grimsby Telegraph* (36) Brian Clark (14, 108), and F Callicott (69). The author has provided the remaining illustrations (4, 5, 45, 47, 51, 52, 66, 78, 79, 92, 103, 106, 112, 122).

Bibliography

Appleby, John (2000) From *Heghelinge to Healing: A Village History*, Albert Gait

Bates, Anderson (1893) *A Gossip About Old Grimsby*, Albert Gait

Boswell, D. and Storey, J. M. (1991 rep) *Grimsby As It Was*, Hendon Publishing Company

Cameron, K. and Field, J. and Insley, J. (1997) *The Place-Names of Lincolnshire: Part Five The Wapentake of Bradley*, English Place-Name Society

Collins, George (1902) *The Brocklesby Hounds*, S Low, Marston & Co

Davies, Revd M., (1942) *The History of Grimsby: From Early Times to the Present Day*, Burnetts Ltd (Grimsby)

Dowling, Alan (2007) *Grimsby Making the Town 1800-1914*, Phillimore

Gillett, Edward (1970) *A History of Grimsby*, Oxford University Press

Gillett, E. Russell, C. and Trevitt, E.H. (1970) *The Enclosures of Scartho, 1795-1798 & Grimsby, 1827-1840*, Grimsby Public Libraries & Museum

Grimsby and Cleethorpes Directory 1860, John Shepherd, Louth

Grimsby (South) 1906 Old Ordnance Survey Map, Published by Alan Godfrey Maps

Grimsby 1903-1908, Cassini Historical Map (2007)

Grimsby 1824, Cassini Historical Map Old Series (2006)

Grimsby Telegraph, 10 May 2010 W*hat's In A Name*

Larn, Graham (2008) *Beer, Hope and Charity*, Century Zero Four Publications

Lincoln, Bob (1913) *The Rise of Grimsby, Vol I*, Farnol, Eades, Irvine and Company

Lincoln, Bob, (1992) *The Rise of Grimsby, Vol II*, Farnol, Eades, Irvine and Company Limited Reprinted by John Rogers, Scartho, Grimsby

Lincolnshire Directory 1826, Whites, Leeds

Mickleburgh, Tim (2005 est.) *Freemo.* (Pamphlet)

Oliver, George (1825) *The Monumental Antiquities of Great Grimsby: An Essay towards ascertaining its origin and ancient population*, Reprinted 2010 by Kessinger Publishing

Oliver, George (1866) *Ye Byrde of Gryme: An Apologue*, Albert Gait

Rigby, S.H., (1993) *Medieval Grimsby: Growth and Decline*, The University of Hull Press

Shaw, George (1897) *Old Grimsby*, Reprinted by Amazon

Streatfield, Rev G.S. (1884) *Lincolnshire and the Danes*, Paul Kegan, Trench and Co.

The News, 5 February 1975 'Hope Street in the bad years started us off.'

Grimsby Evening Telegraph 2 November 1967 'Odd Man Out – Is Saddened as Bulldozers move in at the Abbey'

List of Buildings of Special Architectural or Historic Interest, Department of the Environment, District of Grimsby (31 October 1971)

Grimsby Register of Electors 1901

Local Chronologies from the Grimsby Observer 1880-87

Post Office Directory of Lincolnshire 1855, Kelly and Co., London

Street Index Grimsby Electoral Register 1897

The Universal British Directory, 1790, London

http://www.archive.org/stream/layhavelokdaner00skeagoog/ layhavelokdaner00skeagoog_djvu.txt Accessed 14:00 on 19 July 2011

http://www.batesandmountain.com/history.html Accessed 19:50 on 24 July 2011

http://news.bbc.co.uk/local/northeastwales/hi/people_and_places/history/ newsid_8558000/8558419.stm Accessed 18:12 on 9 August 2011

http://www.cracroftspeerage.co.uk/online/content/index402.htm Accessed 20:45 on 24 July 2011

http://www.cracroftspeerage.co.uk/online/content/index746.htm Accessed 21:59 on 11 August 2011

http://www.uboat.net/wwi/ships_hit/159.html Accessed 14:35 on 9 October 2011

Burkes Peerage

Grimsby & Clee Directory 1893

References

Abbey Road (Rev George Oliver, *Ye Byrde of Gryme* page 139)

Adam Smith Street (Lincoln, Vol II, page 118)

Ainslie Street (Lincoln, Vol II, p 128)

Airedale Way (*Grimsby Evening Telegraph*, 8 December 1973 and 28 February 1974)

Alexandra Road (Lincoln Vol II, p 317)

Alfred Terrace (*Grimsby Evening Telegraph*, 16 May 1986 and 21 June 1972)

Annesley Street (Lincoln Vol II, p 118)

Armstrong Street (Great Grimsby Docks (Royal Dock) Institution of Civil Engineers'
    Transactions, p 46)

Arthur Street (*Grimsby Almanack* 1900–15)

Bemrose Way (*Grimsby Evening Telegraph*, 24 October 1980)

Chantry Lane (Gillett. Lincoln Vol II, p 118)

Charlton Street (*The News*, 28 May 1969)

Convamore Road (Thomas H. Story, *Bartholomew's Gazetteers of the British Isles*, 9th
    edition)

Cromwell Avenue (Lincoln, Vol II, p 352–3; Lincoln, p 126)

Dial Square (Lincoln, *The Rise of Grimsby*, 1913)

Dolby Vale (*Grimsby Evening Telegraph*, 17 March 1947)

Dudley Street (Lincoln, Vol II, p 118)

Eleanor Street (*Grimsby News*, 14 January 1949)

Ethelstone & Fannystone Roads (*Grimsby News*, 1 October 1969)

Farebrother Street (*Grimsby Telegraph*, 29 September 1969)

Freshney Drive (*Grimsby Telegraph*, 9 October 1974)

Garden Street (*Grimsby Evening Telegraph*, 3 November 1941)

Garner Street (*Grimsby Telegraph*, 7 February 1968)

Gilbey Road (*Grimsby Telegraph*, 14 June 2010 'Streets tell of Gilbey's route to success')

Glebe Road *(Grimsby Evening Telegraph*, 1st December 1964)

Hainton Avenue (*Grimsby Observer*, 21 October 1885, 16 October 1889)

Harold Street (Lincoln, Vol II, p 308)

Henry Street (*Grimsby Almanack* 1900–15; Lincoln, Vol II, p 416)

Highfield Avenue (Lincoln, Vol II, p 352-3)

Hilary Road (*Grimsby News*, 15 October 1969)

Hope Street (*Grimsby Free Press & Grimsby Advertiser* 1860; Lincoln, Vol I, p 224)

Hope Street (*Immingham News* 16 June 1967, *The News* 8 October 1968)

Jackson Street (*Grimsby Almanack* 1900–15)

Lambert Road (Lincoln.Vol II, p 266)

Larmour Road (*Grimsby Telegraph*, 6 December 1975)

Nuns' Corner (*The News*, 29 September 1971)

Railway Street (PO Directory of Gy and Clee, 1886)

Rendel Street (Gillett, p 214, *Grimsby Gazette* November 1853)

Richard Street (*Grimsby Evening Telegraph*, 27 March 1975; Grimsby Almanack 1900–1915)

Ropery Street (Lincoln Vol II, pages 289–291)

Tunnard Street (*Grimsby News*, 1 October 1969)

Yarborough Street (Lincoln, Vol II, p 118)

Welhome Road (Lincoln Vol II, page 129)

Wellington Street (Dowling, p 63)